Immigrating and Moving to the USA

A Practical Guide

Compiled and written by

Michael B Dye

and

Jeremy G Stobie

ISBN: 0692263314
ISBN 13: 978-0692263310
Library of Congress Control Number: 2014913450
Blue Pelican Press, Bellevue, WA

FOREWORD

Dear Reader—

The decision to move to the United States is a monumental one, complete with both excitement and challenge. This book has been compiled and written for those of you who are moving to this beautiful melting pot of cultures and individuals that we call the United States of America.

Much of the material in this book was originally produced by the US government and is representative of your tax dollars (or your future tax dollars) at work for you. The rest was written based on our experiences of having the distinct pleasure of helping so many individuals and families move to the United States and make their home here.

We hope that you will find this text useful. Most of all, welcome to the United States of America.

Michael B. Dye, Esq.
Jeremy G. Stobie, CPA, CFE
22 September 2014

HOW TO USE THIS BOOK

While you can certainly read this book cover to cover, it was primarily designed for you to be able to search a topic that you are interested in and read about it.

We suggest that you first read through the table of contents and the index before beginning your reading, as not all of the information contained within the text may be of interest at any given point in time. You can then plan your reading accordingly. The sections related to safety and culture should be read at any stage of your move, and if possible before you move.

The book was also designed to be an ongoing reference as you make your move to and establish yourself in the United States, because you may have questions about visas, taxes, or starting a new business after living in the United States for a period of time.

CONTENTS

Chapter **1**:

IMMIGRATION

a. Visa planning/pre-arrival planning

Requirements for immigrant and nonimmigrant visas

There are two categories of US visas: immigrant and nonimmigrant. Immigrant visas are issued to foreign nationals who intend to live permanently in the United States. Nonimmigrant visas are for foreign nationals wishing to enter the United States on a temporary basis—for tourism, medical treatment, business, temporary work, study, or similar reasons.

Immigrant visa

An immigrant visa is issued to a foreign national who intends to live and work permanently in the United States. In most cases, a relative or employer sponsors the individual by filing an application with US Citizenship and Immigration Services (USCIS). Certain applicants, such as workers with extraordinary ability, investors, and certain special immigrants can petition on their own behalf. The application is later forwarded to the appropriate US consulate or embassy overseas for continued processing and issuance of the immigrant visa to the intending immigrant, if eligible. An intending immigrant must present the immigrant visa at a US port of entry prior to the expiration of the immigrant visa. An intending immigrant becomes a lawful permanent resident once the immigrant visa and accompanying paper work is reviewed and endorsed by a Customs and Border Protection (CBP) officer. For specific information regarding immigrant visa classifications and requirements, refer to the USCIS website (http://www.uscis.gov/) or the Department of State website (http://www.state.gov/).

Family-based immigrant visas

US immigration laws provide a method for a US citizen or lawful permanent resident (LPR) to sponsor the immigration of a family member abroad. The length of time required to complete the process depends on the relationship of the family members, whether the sponsor is a US citizen or an LPR, and sometimes the country where the family member is located.

Immediate relatives: spouse, parent, minor child of adult US citizen (USC). Preference categories:

- FB-1: Unmarried sons/daughters of USCs
- FB-2A: Spouses/minor children of LPRs
- FB-2B: Unmarried children of LPRs
- FB-3: Married sons/daughters of USCs
- FB-4: Brothers/sisters of USCs

Nonimmigrant visa

Nonimmigrant visas are issued to foreign nationals seeking to enter the United States on a temporary basis for tourism, business, medical treatment, and certain types of temporary work. The type of nonimmigrant visa needed is defined by immigration law and related to the purpose of the travel. Generally, an individual applies directly to the US consulate or embassy abroad for a tourist (B-2) or business nonimmigrant (B-1) visa. However, foreign nationals seeking to enter the United States to study or work may require certain authorization and documentation prior to applying for a nonimmigrant visa. For an alphabetical listing of all of the nonimmigrant visa classifications and specific requirements refer to the USCIS website or the US Department of State website.

Issuance of a visa does not guarantee entry to the United States. A visa simply indicates that a US consular officer at an American embassy or consulate has reviewed the application, and that officer has determined that the individual is eligible to enter the country for a specific purpose. The Customs and Border Protection officer at the port of entry will conduct an inspection to determine if the individual is eligible for admission under US immigration law.

Visa-free travel

US policy permits citizens of certain countries as identified below to travel to the United States without a visa. The visa waiver program (VWP) permits nationals from designated countries to apply for admission to the United States for ninety days or less as nonimmigrant visitors for business or pleasure without first obtaining a US nonimmigrant visa.

At the time of application for admission, a VWP applicant must

- be in possession of a round-trip ticket that will transport the individual out of the United States to any other foreign port or place, as long as the trip does not terminate in contiguous territory, and except that the round-trip ticket may transport the traveler to contiguous territory if the traveler is a resident of the country of destination or, if arriving at a land border, provides evidence of financial solvency and a domicile abroad to which the traveler intends to return;
- be arriving on a designated carrier that is signatory to a visa waiver program agreement, if applicable;
- have a machine-readable passport valid for six months beyond the period of intended stay, or essentially nine months (ninety days plus six months). The Department of State's six-month list extending the validity of certain foreign passports can be found on the Department of State website. A traveler with an expired passport is ineligible for VWP admission.
- complete an Arrival/Departure Form I-94W. Travelers arriving at a land border will be required to pay the required Form I-94W processing fee.
- In addition, VWP visitors may not file an application to change status to an immigrant or another nonimmigrant classification or extend their stay beyond the ninety-day time frame. VWP applicants waive their right to proceedings before an immigration Judge, unless they make an asylum application.

Applying for admission into the United States

Q: How does the inspection process work?

A: All persons arriving at a port of entry to the United States are subject to inspection by US Customs and Border Protection (CBP) officers. CBP officers will conduct the immigration, customs, and agriculture components of the inspection process. Additional information regarding the inspection process is located in the Code of Federal Regulations, see e.g. 8 CFR 235 Inspection of Persons Applying for Admission.

Q: Will I be able to travel into or through the United States?

A: Aliens seeking to lawfully enter into the United States must establish their admissibility to the satisfaction of the CBP officer. This is done as part of the inspection process. The reasons that a traveller who is applying for admission into the United States could be inadmissible are found in INA § 212(a).

Q: What procedures apply in considering the health-related grounds of inadmissibility?

Under INA § 212(a)(1)(A), aliens seeking to travel into the United States who have certain health-related issues may be inadmissible. Should it be necessary, a physical and/or mental examination of an applicant for admission should be conducted by a panel physician. When CBP officers encounter an alien at a port of entry who may be inadmissible under public health grounds, the CBP officer may refer the alien to a panel physician. In those circumstances, the CBP officer will provide the alien with the list of panel physicians. In that case, the alien will have to go to one of the panel physicians for an evaluation before again presenting him- or herself for admission. The panel physician will notify CBP of the results of the examination, so that CBP can make an admissibility determination. The panel physician evaluation is valid for only one year. Thus, even if you have previously had such an evaluation, if it has been more than a year since the examination was conducted, a new examination will likely be necessary.

Q: What if I have questions about whether I will be deemed admissible?

A: Before you travel, if you have any concerns about your admissibility, you should seek legal counsel. CBP cannot provide legal advice to members of the public.

Q: What will happen if I am not found admissible?

A: If you are determined to be inadmissible, you could, in certain circumstances, be placed into removal proceedings. In some circumstances an officer may, in his or her sole discretion, determine to permit you to withdraw your application for admission. A determination of inadmissibility may have an impact on your future admissibility and may result in the cancellation of your visa, if you have one.

Prepare for inspection at the US port of entry

During your flight to the United States, flight attendants will give you a CBP Declaration Form 6059B to complete. Air (and sea) arrivals will be posted on an electronic I-94 arrival record available online after inspection is complete at www.cbp.gov/I94.

Land border arrivals may require completing a paper Form I-94 as an arrival record. Use your passport or visa name spelling exactly.

You must present to the US Customs and Border Protection officer your passport with entry visa, your completed Declaration Form 6059B, and any other required documentation related to your travel. You may be asked to show additional documents, such as proof of financial support. Make sure to carry these documents with you, not in your checked baggage. Please see: www.cbp.gov/xp/cgov/travel/id_visa/ for more port-of-entry information.

b. Nonimmigrant visas for business professionals: temporary visitors, business/pleasure (B-1/B-2)

The B visa is the most common type of visa issued worldwide. The flexibility of the B visa allows travelers to temporarily visit the United States for vacation and a multitude of business-related endeavors.

There are three general requirements that an alien must meet in order to qualify for a B visa: (1) The alien must have a foreign residence that the alien intends to maintain; (2) the visit must be temporary, and (3) the visit must be for business (B-1) or pleasure (B-2).

The traveler must not be engaged in any gainful employment (labor for hire) in the United States. The visitor may extend his/her stay or change status to another type of visa. However, no more than one extension on a B-1/B-2 is generally granted, as the visa is for temporary travel to the United States.

A B-1 business visa includes visas to the United States to attend conventions, conferences, consultations, and other legitimate activities of a commercial or professional nature. This may include taking steps to establish a branch office of a foreign company or to set up an investment in the United States.

A B-1 visa is generally granted for a period of entry necessary to conduct one's business.

A B-2 tourist visa includes visits to the United States for pleasure involving recreation, tourism, amusement, visits with friends or relatives, rest, medical treatment, and social networking.

Generally, a B-2 visa will allow the traveler to enter the United States for six months.

c. Other types of visas

Temporary worker visas

Temporary work visas often used by investors and entrepreneurs include the E-1/E-2 treaty trader/treaty investor visas, the L-1 intracompany transferee, H-1B specialist/professional, and the O-1 extraordinary ability visa.

The immigrant investor EB-5 visa, discussed below, is an option for individuals seeking permanent residency (green cards) by investing in the United States.

Nonimmigrant options for investors and entrepreneurs

E-1 and E-2 treaty trader and treaty investor

E-1 treaty traders are persons engaging in substantial trade between the United States and their home country.

Requirements for treaty trader (E-1) include that

- the requisite treaty exists with applicant's country;
- the trading firm for which the applicant is coming to the United States has the nationality of the treaty country;
- that the international trade is substantial, in the sense that there is a sizable and continuing volume of trade;
- the trade is principally between the United States and the treaty country, which is defined to mean that more than 50 percent of the international trade involved must be between the United States and the country of the applicant's nationality;
- the applicant is employed in a supervisory or executive capacity or possesses highly specialized skills essential to the efficient operation of the firm (ordinary skilled or unskilled workers do not qualify); and
- the applicant intends to depart the United States when the E-1 status terminates.

E-2 treaty investors are persons coming to the United States to develop and direct enterprises in the United States in which they are investing a substantial amount of capital.

All types of business ventures qualify, including convenience stores, food franchises, and hotels.

Spouse employment is authorized, and children may attend school. This option may be a viable alternative if the investor is not able to pursue permanent residency under the EB-5 Immigrant Investor program.

Requirements for treaty investor (E-2) include that

- the requisite treaty exists with applicant's country;
- the applicant must be a national of a treaty country;
- the applicant has invested or is in the process of investing;
- the enterprise is a real and operating commercial enterprise;
- the applicant's investment is substantial;
- the investment is more than a marginal one solely for earning a living;
- the applicant is in a position to "develop and direct" the enterprise;
- the applicant, if an employee, is destined to an executive/supervisory position or possesses skills essential to the firm's operations in the United States; and
- the applicant intends to depart the United States when the E-2 status terminates.

L-1 intracompany transferees

This visa category is available for employees who have been employed by a multinational company abroad that seeks to open new business operations in the United States or transfer the employee to an existing business that is related to the company abroad. L-1 regulations also recognize that a visa may be issued for opening a new office.

L-1A for managers/executives
L-1B for employees with specialized company knowledge

H-1B specialist/professional

This visa category is designed to help employers in the United States meet an immediate and temporary need for labor in specialty occupations. A baccalaureate or higher degree or its equivalent is normally the minimum entry requirement.

Jobs in specialty occupations include architecture, engineering, mathematics, physical sciences, social sciences, medicine and health, education, business specialties, accounting, law, theology, and the arts.

There is an annual cap of sixty-five thousand H-1B visas.

O-1 persons with "extraordinary ability"

This applies to the fields of science, art, education, business, and athletics. This visa category is for highly talented or acclaimed foreign nationals who may not qualify in other work-related nonimmigrant categories such as E, H, or L, or who wish to avoid those classifications for various reasons. This visa is especially useful for artists, athletes, entertainers, successful chefs, and businessmen and -women who may be lacking professional degrees.

Temporary (nonimmigrant) workers

In order for you to come to the United States lawfully as a nonimmigrant to work temporarily in the United States, your prospective employer must generally file a nonimmigrant petition on your behalf with USCIS.

Spouses and children seeking dependent nonimmigrant classification

Spouses and children who qualify for dependent nonimmigrant classification of a temporary worker and who are outside of the United States should apply directly at a US consulate for a visa. Spouses and children requesting a change of status or extension of stay in a dependent nonimmigrant classification must file Form I-539, Application to Extend/Change Nonimmigrant Status. Please see the Form I-539 instructions for further information on filing procedures for this application.

Alien federal US tax information

Aliens employed in the United States may have US tax obligations. See the Internal Revenue Service (IRS) for more information.

Temporary worker visa categories: additional information

Important Notice: Effective immediately, US embassies and consulates will adjudicate visa applications that are based on a same-sex marriage in the same way that we adjudicate applications for opposite gender spouses. Please reference the specific guidance on the visa category for which you are applying for more details on documentation required for derivative spouses.

Generally, a citizen of a foreign country who wishes to enter the United States must first obtain a visa—either a nonimmigrant visa for temporary stay or an immigrant visa for permanent residence. Temporary worker visas are for persons who want to enter the United States for employment lasting a fixed period of time and are not considered permanent or indefinite. Each of these visas requires the prospective employer to first file a petition with US Citizenship and Immigration Services (USCIS). An approved petition is required to apply for a work visa.

Labor certification—Some temporary worker visa categories require your prospective employer to obtain a labor certification or other approval from the Department of Labor on your behalf before filing the Petition for a Non-Immigrant Worker, Form I-129, with USCIS. Your prospective employer should review the Instructions for Form I-129 on the USCIS website to determine whether labor certification is required for you.

Petition approval—Some temporary worker categories are limited in total number of petitions that can be approved on a yearly basis. Before you can apply for a temporary worker visa at a US embassy or consulate, a Petition for a Nonimmigrant Worker, Form I-129, must be filed on your behalf by a prospective employer and be approved by USCIS. For more information about the petition process, eligibility requirements by visa category, and numerical limits, visit the I-129 USCIS home page as above. Once the petition is approved, USCIS will send your prospective employer a Notice of Action, Form I-797.

d. Becoming a lawful permanent resident

Your rights and responsibilities

What you do now as a permanent resident can affect your ability to become a US citizen later. The process of becoming a US citizen is called "naturalization."

As a permanent resident, you have the right to

- live and work permanently anywhere in the United States;
- apply to become a US citizen once you are eligible;
- request visas for your husband or wife and unmarried children to live in the United States;
- get Social Security, Supplemental Security Income, and Medicare benefits, if you are eligible;
- own property in the United States;
- apply for a driver's license in your state or territory;
- leave and return to the United States under certain conditions;
- attend public school and college;
- join certain branches of the US Armed Forces;
- purchase or own a firearm, as long as there are no state/local restrictions saying you can't.

As a permanent resident, it is your responsibility to

- obey all federal, state, and local laws;
- pay federal, state, and local income taxes;
- register with the Selective Service (US Armed Forces) if you are a male between ages eighteen and twenty-six (See page 11 for instructions);
- maintain your immigration status;
- carry proof of your permanent resident status at all times.

Change your address online or provide it in writing to the Department of Homeland Security (DHS) within ten days of each time you move.

Permanent residents are issued a valid permanent resident card (Form I-551) as proof of their legal status in the United States. Some people call this a green card. If you are a permanent resident who is eighteen years or older, you must carry proof of your immigration status. You must show it to an immigration officer if asked for it. Your card is valid for ten years and must be renewed before it expires. You should file Form I-90 to replace or renew your permanent resident card. You can get this form at www.uscis.gov or by calling the USCIS Forms Line at (800) 870-3676. There is a fee to file Form I-90.

Your permanent resident card shows that you are allowed to live and work in the United States. You can also use your permanent resident card to reenter the United States. If you are outside the United States for more than twelve months, you will need to show additional documentation to reenter the United States as a permanent resident.

Immigrant visas for business professionals

Immigrant visas are issued to those who intend to reside permanently in the United States (green card holders).Under US law, immigrant visas are generally reserved for individuals who are close relatives of either US citizens or lawful permanent residents (LPRs) in the United States, or for people hired to work in jobs in which it has been determined that there are not enough skilled Americans to perform.

Foreign nationals who are skilled or educated and who have job offers have the possibility of immigrating to the United States. Typically, the prospective employer must first obtain a labor certification and approval of a petition. An approved labor certification (LC) is a document issued by the US Department of Labor (DOL) certifying that

- an employer needs the foreign worker's skills and abilities;
- the employer has tried to recruit US workers for the position;
- the employer has offered the position at the normal or prevailing wage; and
- the employer has found no qualified workers.

EB-1: priority workers

You may be eligible for an employment-based, first-preference visa if you have an extraordinary ability, are an outstanding professor or researcher, or are a multinational executive or manager. Each occupational category has certain requirements that must be met.

EB-2: advanced degree holders and aliens of exceptional ability

You may be eligible for an employment-based, second-preference visa if you are a member of the professions holding an advanced degree or its equivalent or a foreign national who has exceptional ability.

EB-3: professional, skilled, and other workers

You may be eligible for this immigrant-visa preference category if you are a skilled worker, professional, or other worker.

"Skilled workers" are persons whose job requires a minimum of two years of training or work experience, not of a temporary or seasonal nature.

"Professionals" are persons whose job requires at least a US baccalaureate degree or a foreign equivalent and are a member of one of the professions.

The "other workers" subcategory is for persons performing unskilled labor requiring less than two years of training or experience, not of a temporary or seasonal nature.

EB-4: religious workers and other special immigrants

You may be eligible for an employment-based, fourth-preference visa if you are a special immigrant. The following special immigrants are eligible for the fourth-preference visa:

- religious workers
- broadcasters
- Iraqi/Afghan translators
- Iraqis who have assisted the United States
- international organization employees

- physicians
- armed forces members
- Panama Canal Zone E
- retired NATO-6 employees
- spouses and children of deceased NATO-6 employees

EB-5: the "immigrant investor" visa

The US Congress created the EB-5 immigrant visa category in 1990 for immigrants seeking to enter to engage in a commercial enterprise that will benefit the US economy and create at least ten full-time jobs. The basic amount required to invest is $1 million, although that amount may be $500,000 if the investment is made in a "targeted employment area." The US Congress created a temporary pilot program in 1993 that sets aside three thousand visas each year for people who invest in "designated regional centers." Private and governmental agencies may be certified as regional centers if they meet certain criteria.

USCIS administers the Immigrant Investor Program, also known as "EB-5," created by Congress in 1990 to stimulate the US economy through job creation and capital investment by foreign investors. Under a pilot immigration program first enacted in 1992 and regularly reauthorized since, certain EB-5 visas also are set aside for investors in Regional Centers designated by USCIS, based on proposals for promoting economic growth.

All EB-5 investors must invest in a new commercial enterprise that is established after Nov. 29, 1990, or established on or before Nov. 29, 1990, that is

1. Purchased and the existing business is restructured or reorganized in such a way that a new commercial enterprise results, or
2. Expanded through the investment so that a 40 percent increase in the net worth or number of employees occurs.

Commercial enterprise means any for-profit activity formed for the ongoing conduct of lawful business including, but not limited to

- a sole proprietorship;
- partnership (whether limited or general);
- holding company;
- joint venture;
- corporation;
- business trust or other entity that may be publicly or privately owned.

This definition includes a commercial enterprise consisting of a holding company and its wholly owned subsidiaries, provided that each such subsidiary is engaged in a for-profit activity formed for the ongoing conduct of a lawful business.

Note: This definition does not include noncommercial activity such as owning and operating a personal residence.

Job creation requirements

Create or preserve at least ten full-time jobs for qualifying US workers within two years (or under certain circumstances, within a reasonable time after the two-year period) of the immigrant investor's admission to the United States as a conditional permanent resident.

Create or preserve either direct or indirect jobs. Direct jobs are actual identifiable jobs for qualified employees located within the commercial enterprise into which the EB-5 investor has directly invested his or her capital. Indirect jobs are those jobs shown to have been created collaterally or as a result of capital invested in a commercial enterprise affiliated with a regional center by an EB-5 investor. A foreign investor may only use the indirect job calculation if affiliated with a regional center.

Note: Investors may only be credited with preserving jobs in a troubled business.

A troubled business is an enterprise that has been in existence for at least two years and has incurred a net loss during the twelve- or twenty-four-month period prior to the priority date on the immigrant investor's Form I-526. The loss for this period must be at least 20 percent of the troubled business's net worth prior to the loss. For purposes of determining whether the troubled business has been in existence for two years, successors in interest to the troubled business will be deemed to have been in existence for the same period of time as the business they succeeded.

A qualified employee is a US citizen, permanent resident, or other immigrant authorized to work in the United States. The individual may be a conditional resident, an asylee, a refugee, or a person residing in the United States under suspension of deportation. This definition does not include the immigrant investor; his or her spouse, sons, or daughters; or any foreign national in any nonimmigrant status (such as an H-1B visa holder) who is not authorized to work in the United States.

Full-time employment means employment of a qualifying employee by the new commercial enterprise in a position that requires a minimum of thirty-five working hours per week. In the case of the Immigrant Investor Pilot Program, "full-time employment" also means employment of a qualifying employee in a position that has been created indirectly from investments associated with the pilot program.

A job-sharing arrangement whereby two or more qualifying employees share a full-time position will count as full-time employment provided the hourly requirement per week is met. This definition does not include combinations of part-time positions or full-time equivalents even if, when combined, the positions meet the hourly requirement per week. The position must be permanent, full-time, and constant. The two qualified employees sharing the job must be permanent and share the associated benefits normally related to any permanent, full-time position, including payment of both workers' compensation and unemployment premiums for the position by the employer.

Capital investment requirements

Capital means cash, equipment, inventory, other tangible property, cash equivalents, and indebtedness secured by assets owned by the alien entrepreneur, provided that the alien entrepreneur is personally and primarily liable, and that the assets of the new commercial enterprise upon which the petition is based are not used to secure any of the indebtedness. All capital shall be valued at fair-market value in US dollars. Assets acquired, directly or indirectly, by unlawful means (such as criminal activities) shall not be considered capital for the purposes of section 203(b)(5) of the act.

Note: Investment capital cannot be borrowed. Required minimum investments are, in general, $1 million.

Targeted employment areas

In high unemployment or rural areas, the minimum qualifying investment in the United States is $500,000.

A targeted employment area is an area that, at the time of investment, is a rural area or an area experiencing unemployment of at least 150 percent of the national average rate.

A rural area is any area outside a metropolitan statistical area (as designated by the Office of Management and Budget) or outside the boundary of any city or town having a population of twenty thousand or more according to the decennial census.

e. Maintaining permanent residence

Maintaining your permanent resident status

There are some things you must do to maintain your permanent resident status. These are also important to remember if you plan to apply for US citizenship in the future.

Do not leave the United States for an extended period of time or move to another country to live there permanently.

File federal, state and, if applicable, local income tax returns.

Register with the Selective Service, if you are a male between the ages of eighteen and twenty-six.

Give any new address to DHS.

Keep your immigration status. Permanent residents who leave the United States for extended periods, or who cannot show their intent to live permanently in the United States, may lose their permanent resident status. Many immigrants believe they can live abroad as long as they return to the United States at least once a year. This is incorrect. If you think you will be out of the United States for more than twelve months, you should apply for a reentry permit before leaving the country. You should file Form I-131, Application for a Travel Document. You can get this form at www.uscis.gov or by calling the USCIS Forms Line at (800) 870-3676. You must pay a fee to file Form I-131.

A reentry permit is valid for up to two years. You may show the reentry permit, instead of a visa or your permanent resident card, at a port of entry. Having a reentry permit does not guarantee that you will be admitted to the United States when you return, but it can make it easier to show that you are returning from a temporary visit abroad. Visit www.state.gov or your nearest Department of State consular office overseas for more information.

File tax returns

As a permanent resident, you must file income tax returns and report your income to the Internal Revenue Service (IRS) and your state, city, or local tax department, if required. If you do not file income tax returns while living outside of the United States for any length of time, or if you say that you are a "nonimmigrant" on your tax returns, the US government may decide that you have given up your permanent resident status.

Register with the Selective Service

If you are a man and you are eighteen to twenty-six years old, you must register with the Selective Service. When you register, you tell the government that you are available to serve in the US Armed Forces. The United States does not have a military draft now. This means that permanent residents and citizens do not have to serve in the Armed Forces unless they want to. You can register at a US post office or on the Internet. To register for Selective Service on the Internet, visit the Selective Service website: www.sss.gov. To speak with someone from the Selective Service, call (847) 688-6888. This is not a free call. You can also find information on the USCIS website: www.uscis.gov.

Consequences of criminal behavior for permanent residents

The United States is a law-abiding society. Permanent residents in the United States must obey all laws. If you are a permanent resident and engage in or are convicted of a crime in the United States, you could have serious problems. You could be removed from the country, not allowed back into the United States if you leave the country and, in certain circumstances, lose your eligibility for US citizenship. Examples of crimes that may affect your permanent resident status include a crime defined as an "aggravated felony," which includes crimes of violence that are felonies with a one-year prison term or more:

- murder
- terrorist activities
- rape
- sexual assault on a child
- illegal trafficking in drugs, firearms, or people

A crime of "moral turpitude," in general is a crime with an intent to steal or defraud; a crime where physical harm is done or threatened; a crime where serious physical harm is caused by reckless behavior; or a crime of sexual misconduct.

There are also serious consequences for you as a permanent resident if you lie to get immigration benefits for yourself or someone else by

- saying you are a US citizen if you are not;
- voting in a federal election or in a local election open only to US citizens;
- being a "habitual drunkard"—someone who is drunk or uses illegal drugs most of the time;
- being married to more than one person at the same time;

16

- failing to support your family or to pay child or spousal support as ordered;
- being arrested for assaulting or harassing a family member, including violating a protection order—this is called domestic violence;
- lying to get public benefits;
- failing to file tax returns when required;
- willfully failing to register for the Selective Service if you are a male between the ages of eighteen and twenty-six;
- helping someone else who is not a US citizen or national to enter the United States illegally, even if that person is a close relative, and even if you are not paid.

If you have committed or have been convicted of a crime, before you apply for another immigration benefit you should consult with a reputable immigration lawyer or a community-based organization that provides legal service to immigrants.

f. Removal proceedings

The Department of Justice's Executive Office for Immigration Review (EOIR) administers the nation's immigration court system. EOIR primarily decides whether foreign-born individuals, who are charged by the Department of Homeland Security (DHS) with violating immigration law, should be ordered removed from the United States or should be granted relief or protection from removal and be permitted to remain in this country. To make these critical determinations, EOIR's Office of the Chief Immigration Judge (OCIJ) has more than 235 immigration judges who conduct administrative court proceedings, called removal proceedings, in fifty-nine immigration courts nationwide. EOIR's appellate component, the Board of Immigration Appeals (BIA), primarily decides appeals of immigration judge decisions. Certain BIA decisions that the BIA designates as precedent decisions apply to immigration cases nationwide. The BIA is the highest administrative tribunal for interpreting and applying US immigration law.

EOIR's third component, the Office of the Chief Administrative Hearing Officer (OCAHO), hears cases that do not relate to removal proceedings; they relate to employer sanctions for illegal hiring of unauthorized workers, document fraud, and unfair immigration-related employment practices (fact sheet at

www.justice.gov/eoir/press/2012/OCAHOFactSheet05292012.pdf).

g. Immigration court

DHS initiates removal proceedings when it serves the individual with a charging document, called a Notice to Appear, and files that Notice to Appear with one of EOIR's immigration courts. The Notice to Appear orders the individual to appear before an immigration judge and provides notice of the removal proceedings, the alleged immigration law violations, the ability to seek legal representation at no expense to the government, and the consequences of failing to appear at scheduled hearings.

When the immigration court receives the Notice to Appear from DHS, the court schedules a removal hearing before an immigration judge. There may be one or multiple hearings, depending on what happens in the case. The two parties in the hearing are the individual named in the Notice to Appear and DHS.

The DHS attorney represents the government and seeks to prove that the individual should be removed from the United States. The individual in removal proceedings may, at his/her own expense, seek an attorney or other authorized legal representative (fact sheet at:

www.justice.gov/eoir/press/09/WhoCanRepresentAliensFactSheet10022009.pdf)

Removal proceedings begin with a "master calendar" hearing, where the immigration judge ensures the individual understands the alleged immigration law violations. The judge also provides information on available free legal representation resources in the area. Then, generally, the immigration judge will schedule an "individual" hearing, where both parties present the merits of the case to the immigration judge.

The outcome of many removal proceedings depends on whether the individual is eligible for relief from removal. Immigration law provides relief from removal to individuals who meet specific criteria. In most removal proceedings, individuals admit that they are removable, but then they apply for one or more forms of relief. In such cases, individuals must prove that they are eligible for relief, such as cancellation of removal, adjustment of status, asylum, or other remedies provided by immigration law (fact sheet at www.justice.gov/eoir/press/04/ReliefFromRemoval.pdf).

[Caveat Regarding Asylum Claims in the Commonwealth of the Northern Mariana Islands (CNMI)]: Until Jan. 1, 2015, individuals physically present or arriving in the CNMI are not eligible to apply for asylum. These individuals are only eligible to apply for withholding of removal under Section 241(b)(3) of the Immigration and Nationality Act, or withholding of removal under the Convention Against Torture (fact sheet at www.justice.gov/eoir/press/09/AsylumWithholdingCATProtections.pdf).]

Other hearings and reviews

While immigration judges usually conduct removal proceedings, they may also conduct the following hearings and reviews:

Bond redetermination hearings—to determine whether to lower or eliminate the amount of a bond set by DHS for an individual detained by DHS. The detained individual makes a request for a bond redetermination hearing to the immigration judge. These hearings are generally informal and are not part of the removal proceedings.

Rescission hearing—to determine whether a lawful permanent resident should have his/her residency status rescinded because he/she was not entitled to it when it was granted.

Withholding-only hearing—to determine whether an individual who has been ordered removed is eligible for withholding of removal under Section 241(b)(3) of the Immigration and Nationality Act or under the Convention Against Torture.

Asylum-only hearing—to determine whether certain individuals who are not entitled to a removal hearing (crewmen, stowaways, Visa Waiver Pilot Program beneficiaries, and those ordered removed from the United States on security grounds) but claim a well-founded fear of persecution in their home country are eligible for asylum. (See above *Caveat Regarding Asylum Claims in the CNMI.*)

Credible fear review—to determine whether an individual in expedited removal has a credible fear of persecution or torture (fact sheet at www.justice.gov/eoir/press/09/AsylumWithholdingCATProtections.pdf).

Expedited removal allows DHS to remove certain individuals from the United States without placing them in removal proceedings.

Reasonable fear review—to determine whether an individual in expedited removal, who has been previously removed from the United States, has a reasonable fear of persecution or torture (fact sheet at www.justice.gov/eoir/press/09/AsylumWithholdingCATProtections.pdf).

Claimed status review—to determine whether an individual in expedited removal has a valid claim to US citizenship, lawful permanent residency, or refugee or asylum status, when the individual claims under oath to have such status.

In absentia hearing—to determine whether an individual who does not appear for a scheduled hearing may be ordered removed in his/her absence, which is called *in absentia*. The immigration judge will order an individual removed *in absentia* if DHS establishes by clear, unequivocal, and convincing evidence that the individual is removable, and that DHS served the individual with a written notice to appear for the hearing that included information on the consequences of being absent from a hearing.

Immigration judge decisions

At the conclusion of the case, the immigration judge usually issues an oral decision, but on occasion s/he will issue a written decision sometime after the hearing. Immigration judge decisions are made on a case-by-case basis, according to US immigration law, regulations, and precedent decisions. When the immigration judge grants the individual relief from removal, the individual may remain in the United States, sometimes temporarily and sometimes permanently. When the immigration judge orders the individual removed, DHS may remove the individual from the United States. However, an immigration judge's decision may not be the final decision in the case because both parties have the opportunity to appeal an immigration judge's decision in removal proceedings and in the other hearings and reviews specified above.

Appeals of immigration judge decisions—BIA review

Within thirty days of the immigration judge's decision, either party or both parties may appeal the immigration judge's decision to the BIA. The BIA decides the appeal by conducting a "paper" or record review; the BIA, generally, does not conduct courtroom hearings, though it may hold oral argument in selected cases.

Appeals of BIA decisions—federal court review

If the individual in proceedings disagrees with the BIA's ruling, he/she may file an appeal ("petition for review") with the appropriate federal circuit court of appeals. DHS, however, may not do so.

Additional Information:

EOIR's overview fact sheets: www.usdoj.gov/eoir/press/subject.htm

h. Consequences of misrepresentation

Overview

The Immigration and Nationality Act (INA) establishes the types of visas available for travel to the United States and what conditions must be met before an applicant can be issued a particular type of visa. The situations that make a visa applicant ineligible for a visa, called visa ineligibilities, are found in the INA and other immigration laws. The INA also contains provisions for certain ineligible applicants to apply for waivers of their ineligibility.

When a visa applicant applies for a visa, a consular officer at a US embassy or consulate outside the United States determines whether the applicant is qualified, under all applicable US laws, to receive the particular visa applied for. Applicants found qualified are issued visas after all necessary processing is completed. However, when the consular officer determines that the applicant is ineligible to receive a visa, the visa application is denied. The applicant is informed verbally and in writing of the reason for denial based on the applicable section(s) of law.

Review Visa Denials for answers to questions about visa denials, ineligibility, discussion of several ineligibility examples, overcoming visa ineligibility, reapplying for a visa, and waivers of ineligibility. Below is the section of the INA for:

Waivers of Ineligibility

If you are ineligible for a visa based on one or more of the laws listed in Section 212(a) of the Immigration and Nationality Act, you may be able to apply for a waiver. The visa category that you are applying for will determine whether a waiver of ineligibility is available. The consular officer interviewing you will tell you if you may apply for a waiver and will provide detailed instructions for how to apply.

i. Acquiring US citizenship

To become a citizen, you must be willing to swear your loyalty to the United States. You must give up your allegiance to any other country. You must agree to support and defend the US Constitution. When you become a citizen, you accept all of the responsibilities of being an American. In return, you get certain rights and privileges of citizenship.

Why become a US citizen?

Permanent residents have most of the rights of US citizens. But there are many important reasons to consider becoming a US citizen. Here are some good reasons:

- Becoming a citizen is a way to demonstrate your commitment to your new country.
- Only citizens can vote in federal elections. Most states also restrict the right to vote, in most elections, to US citizens.
- Serving on a jury. Only US citizens can serve on a federal jury. Most states also restrict jury service to US citizens. Serving on a jury is an important responsibility for US citizens.
- When you travel with a US passport, it enables you to get assistance from the US government when overseas, if necessary.
- US citizens generally get priority when petitioning to bring family members permanently to this country.

- In most cases, a child born abroad to a US citizen is automatically a US citizen.
- Certain jobs with government agencies require US citizenship.
- Only citizens can run for federal office (US Senate or House of Representatives) and for most state and local offices.
- A US citizen's right to remain in the United States cannot be taken away.
- You become eligible for federal grants and scholarships. Many financial aid grants, including college scholarships and funds given by the government for specific purposes, are available only to US citizens.
- Some government benefits are available only to US citizens.

Naturalization: becoming a citizen

The process of becoming a US citizen is called "naturalization." You can apply for naturalization once you meet the following requirements:

- live in the United States for at least five years as a permanent resident (or three years if married to and living with a US citizen)
- are present in the United States for at least thirty months out of the past five years (or eighteen months out of the past three years if married to and living with a US citizen)
- Llive within a state or USCIS district for at least three months before you apply You may have to follow different rules if
  - you, or your deceased parent, spouse, or child, have served in the US Armed Forces;
  - you are a US national;
  - you obtained permanent residence through the 1986 amnesty law;
  - you are a refugee or asylum seeker;
  - you have a US citizen spouse who is regularly stationed abroad;
  - you lost US citizenship under prior law because of marriage to a noncitizen;
  - you are an employee of certain types of companies or nonprofit organizations.

Getting naturalization information

People eighteen years or older who want to become citizens should get Form M-476, *A Guide to Naturalization*. This guide has important information on the requirements for naturalization. It also describes the forms you will need to begin the naturalization process.

To see if you are eligible to apply for naturalization, see Form M-480, Naturalization Eligibility Worksheet, at the end of *A Guide to Naturalization*. Use Form N-400 to apply for naturalization. There is a fee to file Form N-400.

To get Forms M-476, M-480, and N-400, call the USCIS Forms Line at (800) 870-3676 or get them from www.uscis.gov. Consult *A Guide to Naturalization* for more information. You may also wish to consult an immigration attorney or other qualified professional.

Requirements for naturalization

The general requirements for naturalization are

- living in the United States as a permanent resident for a specific amount of time (continuous residence);
- being present in the United States for specific time periods (physical presence);
- spending specific amounts of time in your state or USCIS district (time in state or USCIS district);
- behaving in a legal and acceptable manner (good moral character);
- knowing English and information about US history and government (English and civics);
- understanding and accepting the principles of the US Constitution (attachment to the Constitution).

Continuous residence

"Continuous residence" means that you must live in the United States as a permanent resident for a certain period. If you leave the United States for more than six months, your residence status is possibly broken. If you leave the United States for more than one year, your residence status *is* broken. Most people must be permanent residents in continuous residence for five years (or three years if married to a US citizen) before they can begin the naturalization process. For refugees, this means five years from the date you arrived in the United States, which is usually the date you obtained permanent resident status. For those granted asylum status in the United States, this period begins one year before you got permanent resident status. The date on your permanent resident card is the date your five years begins. If you leave the United States for a long time, usually six months or more, you may "break" your continuous residence. To keep your status, you must prove that you continued to live, work, and/or have ties to the United States (e.g., paid taxes) while you were away. In most cases, you must begin your continuous residence over. Apply for a reentry permit before you leave if you plan to return to the United States as a permanent resident.

Exemptions for one-year absences

If you work for the US government, a recognized US research institution, or certain US corporations, or if you are a member of the clergy serving abroad, you may be able to preserve your continuous residence if you have been physically present and living in the United States without leaving for at least one year after becoming a permanent resident. Submit Form N-470, Application to Preserve Residence for Naturalization Purposes, before you have been outside the United States for one year. There is a fee to file Form N-470.

For more information, contact the USCIS forms line at: (800) 870-3676 and ask for Form N-470, Application to Preserve Residence for Naturalization Purposes. You can also get the form on the USCIS website at www.uscis.gov.

TIP: A reentry permit (Form I-131) and the Application to Preserve Residence for Naturalization Purposes (Form N-470) are not the same. You may show a reentry permit instead of your permanent resident card (if you have been gone for less than twelve months) or instead of a visa (if you have been gone for more than twelve moths) when you return to the United States after a temporary absence.

If you leave the United States for one year or longer, you may be able to return if you have a reentry permit. You should apply for this reentry permit before you depart the United States. In most cases, none of the time you were in the United States before you left the country will count toward your time in continuous residence. This means that you will need to begin your continuous residence again after you return to the United States, and you may have to wait up to four years and one day before you can apply for naturalization.

Exemptions for military personnel

If you are on active-duty status or were recently discharged from the US Armed Forces, the continuous residence and physical presence requirements may not apply to you. You can find more information in the M-599 Naturalization Information for Military Personnel brochure. Every military base should have a point of contact to handle your naturalization application and certify a Form N-426, Request for Certification of Military or Naval Service. You must submit Form N-426 with your application forms. To get the forms you need, call the USCIS toll-free military help line at (877) CIS-4MIL (877) 247-4645). You can find more information at www.uscis.gov/military or by calling customer service at (800) 375-5283.

Be aware that absences from the United States while your naturalization application is pending could cause problems with your eligibility, especially if you accept employment abroad.

Physical presence in the United States

Physical presence means that you actually have been present in the United States. If you are a permanent resident at least eighteen years old, you must be physically present in the United States for at least thirty months during the last five years (or eighteen months during the last three years, if married to a US citizen) before you apply for naturalization.

Q: What is the difference between physical presence and continuous residence?
A: Physical presence is the total days you were inside the United States and does not include the time you spend outside the United States. Each day you spend outside the United States takes away from your physical presence total. If you are away from the United States for long periods of time or if you take many short trips outside the United States, you may not meet your physical presence requirement. To count your physical presence time, you should add together all the time you have been in the United States. Then subtract all trips you have taken outside the United States. This includes short trips to Canada and Mexico. For example, if you go to Mexico for a weekend, you must include the trip when counting how many days you spent out of the country.

Continuous residence is the total time you have resided as a permanent resident in the United States before applying for naturalization. If you spend too much time outside the United States during a single trip, you may break your continuous residence.

j. Time as a resident in state or USCIS district

Most people must live in the state or USCIS district where they apply for naturalization for at least three months. Students can apply for naturalization either where they go to school or where their family lives (if they depend on their parents for support).

Behaviors that might show a lack of good moral character include

- drunk driving or being drunk most of the time;
- illegal gambling;

- prostitution;
- lying to gain immigration benefits;
- failing to pay court-ordered child support;
- committing terrorist acts;
- persecuting someone because of race, religion, national origin, political opinion, or social group.

To be eligible for naturalization, you must be a person of good moral character. A person is not considered to be of "good moral character" if they commit certain crimes during the five years before they apply for naturalization or if they lie during their naturalization interview.

If you commit some specific crimes, you can never become a US citizen and will probably be removed from the country. These crimes are called "bars" to naturalization. Crimes called "aggravated felonies" (if committed on or after November 29, 1990), including murder, rape, sexual abuse of a child, violent assault, treason, and illegal trafficking in drugs, firearms, or people are some examples of permanent bars to naturalization. In most cases, immigrants who were exempted or discharged from serving in the US Armed Forces because they were immigrants, and immigrants who deserted from the US Armed Forces, are also permanently barred from US citizenship.

You also may be denied citizenship if you behave in other ways that show you lack good moral character. Other crimes are temporary bars to naturalization. Temporary bars usually prevent you from becoming a citizen for up to five years after you commit the crime. These include:

- any crime against a person with intent to harm;
- any crime against property or the government involving fraud;
- two or more crimes with combined sentences of five years or more;
- violating controlled substance laws (e.g., using or selling illegal drugs);
- spending 180 days or more during the past five years in jail or prison.

Report any crimes that you committed when you apply for naturalization. This includes crimes removed from your record or committed before your eighteenth birthday. If you do not tell USCIS about them, you may be denied citizenship, and you could be prosecuted.

English and civics

In general, you must show that you can read, write, and speak basic English. You also must have a basic knowledge of US history and government (also known as civics). You will be required to pass a test of English and a test of civics to prove your knowledge. Many schools and community organizations help people prepare for their citizenship tests. You can find examples of test questions in *A Guide to Naturalization*. *The* USCIS Office of Citizenship offers products, such as the Civics Flash Cards and *Learn about the United States: Quick Civics Lessons* to help you study. You can get these for free at www.uscis.gov.

Attachment to the Constitution

You must be willing to support and defend the United States and its Constitution. You declare your attachment, or loyalty, to the United States and the Constitution when you take the oath of citizenship.

Exemptions to the English and civics requirements

Some people who apply for naturalization have different test requirements because of their age and the length of time they have lived in the United States.

If you are age fifty, fifty-five, or sixty-five or older, depending on category, or you have lived as permanent resident in the United States for ten years, fifteen years, or twenty years, you do not take the English test, but you must take the simplified civics test in your language.

If you do not have to take the English test, you must bring your own translator for the civics test. Under certain circumstances, if you have a disability that makes it impossible for you to come to an interview, special arrangements may be made. To get more information, contact the USCIS Forms Line at (800) 870-3676 and ask for Form N-648 or get a copy from the USCIS website at www.uscis.gov.

You become a US citizen when you take the oath of citizenship.

People who show they have a physical or developmental disability that makes them unable to understand the meaning of the oath do not have to take the oath of citizenship.

If you have a pending naturalization application, and you move, you must notify USCIS of your new address. You can call (800) 375-5283 to report your new address. You must also file Form AR-11 with DHS. You may change your address online via an electronic AR-11 form at www.uscis.gov. See page 12 for instructions.

Naturalization ceremonies

If USCIS approves your application for naturalization, you must attend a ceremony and take the oath of citizenship. USCIS will send you a Form N-445, Notice of Naturalization Oath Ceremony, to tell you the time and date of your ceremony. You must complete this form and bring it to your ceremony.

You are not a citizen until you have taken the oath of citizenship. An official will read each part of the oath slowly and ask you to repeat the words. After you take the oath, you will receive your certificate of naturalization. This certificate proves that you are a US citizen. You are not a citizen until you have taken the oath of citizenship at a formal naturalization ceremony.

The oath of citizenship ceremony is a public event. Many communities hold special ceremonies on Independence Day, July 4, of each year. Check to see if your community holds a special July Fourth citizenship ceremony and how you can participate. Many people bring their families and celebrate after the ceremony.

k. Renouncing US citizenship

Overview

Section 349(a)(5) of the Immigration and Nationality Act (INA) (8 USC 1481(a)(5)) is the section of law that governs the ability of a United States citizen to renounce his or her US citizenship. That section of law provides for the loss of nationality by voluntarily performing the following act with the intent to relinquish his or her US nationality by: "(5) making a formal renunciation of nationality before a diplomatic or consular officer of the United States in a foreign state, in such form as may be prescribed by the Secretary of State."

Elements of renunciation

A person wishing to renounce his or her US citizenship must voluntarily and with intent to relinquish US citizenship appear in person before a US consular or diplomatic officer in a foreign country (normally at a US embassy or consulate) and sign an oath of renunciation.

Renunciations that do not meet the conditions described above have no legal effect. Because of the provisions of section 349(a)(5), Americans cannot effectively renounce their citizenship by mail, through an agent, or while in the United States. In fact, US courts have held certain attempts to renounce US citizenship to be ineffective on a variety of grounds, as discussed below.

Requirement—Renounce all rights and privileges

In the case of Colon v. US Department of State, 2 F.Supp.2d 43 (1998), plaintiff was a United States citizen and resident of Puerto Rico, who executed an oath of renunciation before a consular officer at the US embassy in Santo

Domingo. The district court for the District of Columbia rejected Colon's petition for a writ of mandamus directing the secretary of state to approve a Certificate of Loss of Nationality in the case, because the plaintiff wanted to retain one of the primary benefits of US citizenship while claiming he was not a US citizen. The court described the plaintiff as a person "claiming to renounce all rights and privileges of US citizenship, [while] plaintiff wants to continue to exercise one of the fundamental rights of citizenship, namely to travel freely throughout the world and, when he wants to, return and reside in the United States." See also Jose Fufi Santori v. United States of America, 1994 US App. LEXIS 16299 (1994) for a similar case. A person who wants to renounce US citizenship cannot decide to retain some of the privileges of citizenship, as this would be logically inconsistent with the concept of renunciation. Thus, such a person can be said to lack a full understanding of renouncing citizenship and/or lack the necessary intent to renounce citizenship, and the Department of State will not approve a loss of citizenship in such instances.

Dual nationality/statelessness

Persons intending to renounce US citizenship should be aware that, unless they already possess a foreign nationality, they may be rendered stateless and, thus, lack the protection of any government. They may also have difficulty traveling as they may not be entitled to a passport from any country. Even if they were not stateless, they would still be required to obtain a visa to travel to the United States or show that they are eligible for admission pursuant to the terms of the Visa Waiver Pilot Program (VWPP). If found ineligible for a visa or the VWPP to come to the United States, a renunciant, under certain circumstances, could be barred from entering the United States. Nonetheless, renunciation of US citizenship may not prevent a foreign country from deporting that individual back to the United States in some noncitizen status.

Tax and military obligations/No escape from prosecution

Also, persons who wish to renounce US citizenship should also be aware that the fact that a person has renounced US citizenship may have no effect whatsoever on his or her US tax or military service obligations (contact the Internal Revenue Service or US Selective Service for more information). In addition, the act of renouncing US citizenship will not allow persons to avoid possible prosecution for crimes that they may have committed in the United States or escape the repayment of financial obligations previously incurred in the United States or incurred as US citizens abroad.

Renunciation for minor children

Parents cannot renounce US citizenship on behalf of their minor children. Before an oath of renunciation will be administered under Section 349(a)(5) of the INA, a person under the age of eighteen must convince a US diplomatic or consular officer that he/she fully understands the nature and consequences of the oath of renunciation, is not subject to duress or undue influence, and is voluntarily seeking to renounce his/her US citizenship.

Irrevocability of renunciation

Finally, those contemplating a renunciation of US citizenship should understand that the act is irrevocable, except as provided in section 351 of the INA (8 USC 1483) and cannot be canceled or set aside absent successful administrative or judicial appeal. (Section 351(b) of the INA provides that an applicant who renounced his or her US citizenship before the age of eighteen can have that citizenship reinstated if he or she makes that desire known to the Department of State within six months after attaining the age of eighteen. See also Title 22, Code of Federal Regulations, section 50.20).

Renunciation is the most unequivocal way in which a person can manifest an intention to relinquish US citizenship. Please consider the effects of renouncing US citizenship, described above, before taking this serious and irrevocable action.

Chapter 2:

MOVING TO THE UNITED STATES

a. Deciding where to live

Once you have decided to move to the United States, you will then need to decide exactly where to live. This decision should be taken with reasonable care, and it is best to make a final decision once you have arrived—if possible, find temporary housing until you can make a decision—and have spent some time in a given location.

If you are relocating due to a job, and you need to take up residence close to work, you will have a general idea of where to live. However, bear in mind that local traffic patterns and other elements can make a large difference between the commute time from one seemingly close location to another.

If you are buying a home, it is even more important to take your time and understand the local market, traffic patterns, distance to schools, quality of schools (this is one of the main drivers of real estate value in the United States), and major employers in the area.

Taxes are also an important consideration of where to live in the United States, as state and city taxes can vary widely.

b. Bringing your things

Shipping or transporting items from your home country to the United States can be expensive. The less that you bring the easier and less expensive your move will be. It is a good idea to determine what items you might not be able to replace or purchase in the United States when deciding what items to bring. Then ship only those items.

Electronic items may or may not work in the United States as outlets supply electricity at 120 volts at 60 Hertz, which is different than many other countries (you can check to see if your electronics will work with US outlets at the following: www.electricaloutlet.org).

Keep in mind that US Customs may search anything that you bring into the United States, and it is a good idea to research whether the items that you are bringing into the United States are allowable (for example, medicines, plants, animals, and food).

If you are bringing a large amount of cash or negotiable monetary instruments— i.e., currency, personal checks (endorsed), traveler's checks, gold coins, or securities or stocks in bearer form—valued at $10,000 or more, you will need to complete and submit a form FinCEN 105 (http://www.fincen.gov/fin105_cmir.pdf) to a US Customs and Border Protection office upon your entry to the United States.

c. Renting or buying a home

Both renting and buying have advantages and disadvantages. Some advantages of renting include being generally free of most maintenance responsibilities, and having the freedom to move (at the end of the lease term) without relying on the real estate market to sell your home. With renting, however, you lose the chance to build equity, take advantage of tax benefits, and protect yourself against rent increases. Also, you may not be free to decorate without permission, and you may be at the mercy of the landlord in a tight rental market.

Owning a home also has benefits. When you make a mortgage payment, you are building equity. And that's an investment. Owning a home also qualifies you for tax breaks that assist you in dealing with your new financial responsibilities, such as insurance, real estate taxes, and upkeep, which can be substantial.

Renting a home

Apartments and houses can be rented. You can find these in several ways:

- Look for "Apartment Available" or "For Rent" signs on buildings.
- Look in the newspaper in the section called "Classified Advertisements" or "Classifieds." Find the pages listing "Apartments for Rent" and "Homes

for Rent." These will have information about homes, such as where they are located, the number of rooms, and the cost of rent.

- Ask friends and relatives or people at your job if they know of places to rent.
- Check bulletin boards in libraries, grocery stores, and community centers for "For Rent" notices.
- Check for rentals online. If you don't have a computer at home, you can go to your local public library or an Internet café.
- Call a local real estate agent.

What to expect when you rent a home:

Applying to Rent—People who rent out apartments or homes are called landlords. A landlord may ask you to fill out a rental application form. This is so the landlord can check to see if you have the money to pay the rent. The application form may ask for a Social Security number and proof that you are working. You can use your permanent resident card if you do not have a Social Security number yet. You can also show a pay stub from your job to prove you are working. You may also be asked to pay a small application fee.

If you are not yet working, you may need someone to sign the rental agreement with you. This person is called a "cosigner." If you cannot pay the rent, the cosigner will have to pay the rent for you.

Signing a Lease—You sign a rental agreement or "lease" if the landlord agrees to rent to you. When you sign a lease, you agree to pay your rent on time and stay for a specific length of time. Most leases are for one year. You can also find housing for shorter periods of time, such as one month. You may have to pay more money for a short lease than for a longer one.

When you sign a lease, you agree to keep the home clean and in good shape. You may be charged extra if you damage the place you are renting. The lease may also list the number of people who can live in the home.

A lease is a legal document. You must keep up your part of the agreement. Landlords must also do their part. They must keep the property safe and in good condition.

Paying a security deposit—Renters usually pay a security deposit when they move in. This deposit is usually equal to one month's rent. You will get this deposit back if the home is clean and in good condition when you move out. If not, the landlord may keep some or all of your deposit to pay for cleaning or repairs. Inspect the house or apartment before you move in. Tell the landlord about any problems you find. Talk to your landlord before you move out to find out what you need to fix to get all of your security deposit back.

Paying other rental costs—For some houses or apartments, the rent payment includes the cost of utilities (gas, electricity, heat, water, and trash removal). For other rentals, you must pay separately for these expenses. Ask the landlord if utilities are included when you are looking for housing. If they are, make sure this is in your rental agreement before you sign it. If utilities are not included, you should find out how much they will cost. The cost of some utilities will be more in the summer (for air conditioning) or winter (for heat).

Ending a lease—Ending a rental agreement is called terminating your lease. Your landlord may agree to terminate your lease early if he or she can find someone else to rent your home. If not, you may have to pay monthly rent until the end of the lease, even if you are not living there. You also may lose your security deposit if you leave before the end of the lease.

Give your landlord a written notice that you want to move out. Most landlords require notice at least thirty days before you want to leave.

Buying a home

For many people owning a home is part of the American Dream. Owning a home has many benefits, and it brings many responsibilities.

Real estate agents can help you find a home to buy. Ask friends or coworkers, or call a local real estate agency for the name of an agent. Ask for an agent who knows the area where you want to buy your house. You can look in the newspaper "Classifieds" under "Homes for Sale." You can also look for "For Sale" signs in the neighborhoods you like.

Most people need to get a loan to pay for a home; this is called a mortgage. You can get a mortgage from a local bank or from a mortgage company. Getting a mortgage means you are borrowing money at a specific rate of interest for a specific period of time. Interest you pay on your mortgage can be deducted from your federal income tax.

You also need to obtain homeowners insurance to help pay for any possible future damage to your home. Insurance usually covers damage due to bad weather, fire, or robbery.

You will also need to pay property taxes on the value of your home.

A real estate agent or real estate lawyer can help you obtain a mortgage and insurance. He or she can also help you fill out the forms to buy your home. A real estate agent should not charge you a fee to buy a home. But you may have to pay a fee to a real estate lawyer to help you fill out the forms. You will also have to pay fees to get your mortgage and to file legal forms with the state. These fees are called "closing costs." Your real estate agent or mortgage lender must tell you how much these fees will be before you sign the final purchase forms for your home.

Home cost differences

Home costs vary widely in the United States. Prices for a similar-size home in one section of a city may be vastly different from prices in another section of a city and even significantly different from one neighborhood to another.

The best way to establish an understanding of home prices in a certain location is to spend time there, look at real estate listings, drive through neighborhoods, and compare costs.

Home size in the United States vs. international

Homes in the United States are generally larger than in many other countries. This is due to an abundance of land and an expectation from the American consumer that "bigger is better." A comparison between international average home sizes is listed below:

United States: 2,300 square feet
Australia: 2,217 square feet
Denmark: 1,475 square feet
France: 1,216 square feet
Spain: 1,044 square feet
Ireland: 947 square feet
United Kingdom: 818 square feet
(data from: www.apartmenttherapy.com)

What makes an American home different?

Aside from the fact that American homes are usually much larger than homes in many countries, you may find that there are many other differences between an average American home and one that you might be used to. These might include the following:

- Most American homes have central heating and air conditioning, controlled by thermostats located throughout the house (this may not be the case in climates where it is not necessary).
- Most American homes do not use the burning of wood to heat the home; the fireplace is usually decorative.

- The walls of an American home are usually made out of drywall and wood, not concrete.
- Many American homes have garden areas and grassy yards, which you will water with drinking water.
- Many American homes do not have gates or bars on the doors and windows.
- Most American homes have a washer and a dryer, and it is now rare to dry your clothing outside.

You will be expected to maintain your own house to the standards of the community.

Property taxes and costs of ownership

Property taxes are taxes on the value of your property. Property taxes are a major source of revenues for state and local governments. Property tax rates vary by location and can be more than 2.5 percent of the appraised value of your property on an annual basis. If you do not pay your property taxes on time, you may be faced with fines and penalties, and you can also have your property foreclosed on by the taxing authority (where they will take the property and sell it in satisfaction of your tax debt). It is very important to understand what property taxes you will be responsible for prior to purchasing your home or property.

Other costs of ownership can include maintenance and repairs, utilities, pest control, insurance, and homeowners/condominium association fees. These costs can be significant and can amount to over 5 percent of the value of your home on an annual basis.

Homeowners (and condo owners) associations

A homeowners' or condominium owners' association is an organization for a neighborhood, subdivision, building, or community that makes and enforces rules for the properties in its jurisdictions. The association collects monthly or annual dues to pay for the maintenance of the common areas (such as entrances, pools, playgrounds, lobbies, elevators, etc.). These associations can level special assessments to pay for major repairs or improvements, and they may have the ability to foreclose on your property if you do not pay the dues.

d. Insurance

It is likely that your home will be your biggest asset in the United States, and it should be insured against risk of loss from fire or other disaster. This type of insurance is commonly called homeowners insurance and (depending on the insurer) will usually compensate you for losses to your possessions in your home—and your home itself in the event of loss. It can protect you from losses caused by fire, theft, storms, and other natural disasters (make sure that your policy covers a specific type of disaster, as you may need additional earthquake or flood insurance).

Insurance premiums (the cost of the insurance) are based on the construction of the home, the value of the home, the area where the home is located, and other risks. Premiums are either paid on an annual, monthly, or quarterly basis.

It is a good idea when shopping for homeowners insurance that you compare coverage and costs, as they can vary widely. Some major insurance companies that provide this type of insurance are listed below (Note: this is not an exhaustive list, just a place for you to start comparison):

Progressive Insurance (www.progressive.com)
Allstate (www.allstate.com)
Farmers (www.farmers.com)
Liberty Mutual (www.libertymutual.com)
Geico (www.geico.com)
Nationwide (www.nationwide.com)

e. Moving in the United States

Moving inside of the United States is relatively simple. Aside from any notification requirements that you may have with USCIS, you do not need any approval or other authorization to move from city to city or into a different state. Keep in mind that when you move, you may be subject to new or different taxes in your new resident state/city, so it is a good idea to find out what your obligations may be prior to moving.

You also need to check with the local driver's license office in the location that you are moving to and find out their requirements for obtaining a driver license in that state and when you must do this.

When moving your things you can either hire a moving company to move them for you, or you can rent a large vehicle and move them yourself.

f. Selling your home

When you decide to sell your home, you can either hire a real estate agent or try to do it yourself. If you are selling your home for the first time, and you are not aware of the process and requirements, it is a good idea to hire a real estate agent.

Aside from helping you understand the process and managing this process for you, the real estate agent also "lists" the property and makes this listing available to other agents, who may have clients looking to purchase a property like yours.

The best place to find a good real estate agent (or Realtor) is through recommendations from your friends and family. If you do not know anyone in a specific market, you can check the local association of real estate agents to find contact information for real estate agents in your area. You can also check listings for properties that are in the same area and price range of your home and research these real estate agents.

If possible, try to check reviews for the particular real estate agents online before scheduling a meeting. Selecting a real estate agent is an important decision and a highly personal process, and you should interview several potential real estate agents before making a final selection.

Chapter 3:

THE UNITED STATES AT A GLANCE—LIFE IN AMERICA

a. Living in the United States

This guide will help you get started, but it cannot answer all the questions you have about life in the United States. To find additional information, you may wish to contact a state, county, or city government office to learn about services you need or consult with a local organization that helps new immigrants settle into life here. You can find these offices and organizations by using the free resources described below.

Forming relationships with people who have also moved to the United States will be helpful. It is likely that they have had the same or similar experiences and can help by providing advice as to how to best adapt to your new home.

The Public Library

Public libraries in the United States are free and open to everyone. Libraries are located in almost every community. The library staff can help you find information on almost any topic and can give you a library card that allows you to borrow items, such as books and videotapes, free of charge. Most libraries also have local newspapers for you to read and computers that you can use to search the

Internet. Ask the library staff to show you how to use the computer to search the Internet. Some libraries give free classes on how to search the Internet. Some libraries also provide English language tutoring or classes and other programs for children and adults.

The Internet

The Internet can link you to many sources of information, including the websites of federal, state, and local government agencies. Most government websites end with ".gov." If you do not have a computer at home, you can use one in your public library or at an Internet café, which is a business that charges a fee for using a computer with Internet service. You can use the Internet to search for jobs, find housing, learn about schools for your children, and locate community organizations and resources to help you. You can also find important news and current events and discover interesting information on the Internet about life in America, US history and government, and your local community. **Visit www. welcometousa.gov to locate all federal government resources available to new immigrants.**

TIP: As an immigrant, you should be aware that dishonest people have made websites that look like government websites to confuse you and take advantage of you. Remember that www.uscis.gov is the official website of US Citizenship and Immigration Services.

Community and faith-based organizations that assist immigrants

There are organizations in many communities that provide free or very low-cost assistance to immigrants. These organizations can help you learn about your community and the services available to you as an immigrant. You can look for these organizations by searching on the Internet.

Language (slang, accents)

English is the language spoken by most people in the United States. The official language of many states is English, and it is the language used in nearly all governmental functions. Despite this predominance, many people in the United States speak languages other than English. According to the US Census Bureau, 2011 American Community Survey, of 291.5 million people aged five and over, 60.6 million people (21 percent of this population) spoke a language other than English at home. A list of seventeen of the common languages other than English spoken in the home for the period 1980–2010 includes Spanish or Spanish Creole, French (including Patois, Cajun, Creole), Italian, Portuguese or Portuguese Creole,

German, Yiddish, Greek, Russian, Polish, Serbo-Croatian, Armenian, Persian, Chinese, Japanese, Korean, Vietnamese, and Tagalog.

English language classes are available to students from all over the world, and they are easily located in every state and major city throughout the United States.

- English as a Second Language, or ESL, programs offer international students the chance to learn English or improve their English language skills. Courses are offered at hundreds of US educational institutions and range from academic English for university-bound students to language and culture courses for travelers.
- Intensive English Programs (IEPs) can also be taken for personal or professional reasons and not for academic credit. They may also be taken to prepare for US college or university admissions, and some IEPs offer "bridge programs" that help students transfer into an academic program. IEPs may include classes designed for any level of English proficiency and usually require twenty to thirty hours per week of intensive English language study.

Customs

American culture reflects many of the customs and traditions of the United States, including language, etiquette, religion, food, and the arts. Nearly every region of the world has influenced American culture, as it is a country of immigrants, most notably the English who colonized the country beginning in the early sixteen hundreds.

The United States is sometimes described as a "melting pot," in which different cultures have contributed their own distinct "flavors" to American culture. Just as cultures from around the world have influenced American culture, today American culture influences the world. The term "Western culture" often refers broadly to the cultures of the United States and Europe. Some American customs may seem strange to people from other countries, but knowing about them may help you better adapt during your stay in the United States.

a. Being on time is important.
b. Americans like privacy and personal space (which means that most Americans will keep their distance from you when first meeting).
c. Americans can be very direct and honest, even though it may seem rude to people from another culture.
d. Americans ask about how your day is going without expecting an answer.

e. Americans value independent thinking.

f. Americans like to joke, smile, and talk.

g. Americans are very concerned with personal hygiene and cleanliness. It is not unusual for them to bathe one or even two times a day.

h. Getting in line—Always get in line and wait your turn when buying tickets or waiting in a bank, a post office, or for a bus or train. It is considered rude to cut in line. If there is any confusion about whether there is one line or more for several different cashiers, you should still wait your turn and stay behind everyone who arrived before you. Americans do not try to get to the front first; they are very fair. You will often hear people saying, "Who's next?" The general rule is that you are next if you were the first person to have gotten in line.

i. Smoking—Smoking indoors in public places is illegal in many cities and states in the United States. There are even certain areas outdoors, such as near building entrances, where smoking is prohibited.

j. Drugs—Buying and selling illicit drugs is illegal in the United States. If you are found carrying drugs either in school or in public, you may be arrested.

k. Women—Women in the United States are seen as equal to men and should be treated fairly. It is normal for men and women to do an equal share of the household tasks and child care. This may not be the case in certain more traditional American families, and every couple has their own arrangement.

l. Safety for women—It is not a good idea for women to walk around on their own at night. Make sure that you use registered taxis and try to stay with a group as much as possible.

m. Personal hygiene
    *   Restrooms—It is customary to flush the toilet after use and to dispose of toilet paper in the toilet. Ladies' sanitary napkins should, however, be placed in the trash can.
    *   Tissues—It is the American custom to blow one's nose with a tissue. Some people keep a tissue or a handkerchief up their sleeve or in their pocket.
    *   Spitting—In the United States, it is rude to spit in public.
    *   Water—The water in the taps is clean enough to drink and brush your teeth with. Some people prefer to drink bottled water, and some people filter their water in a pitcher before they drink it.

n. Mealtimes—Most Americans eat three times a day. Breakfast can be a small meal of cereal, toast, or some fruit, or a more substantial cooked breakfast of eggs, bacon, or omelets, according to preference. People in the United States usually eat a light lunch—soup, sandwiches, or a salad are the most common foods chosen for a weekday lunch. This is normally eaten between noon and 2:00 p.m.

o. In the United States, the evening meal is usually eaten between 5:30 p.m. and 7:30 p.m. This is usually called "dinner." It is normally a large meal consisting of meat or fish and vegetables, or a dish made with eggs, pasta, or pizza.

p. Eating in restaurants—Americans are very polite to waiters in restaurants. If you want a waiter to come to your table, you should raise your hand, but not snap your fingers. To attract their attention when they are close by, you should say, "Excuse me."

q. American table manners and customs—If you put your knife and fork on your plate, a waiter will think that you have finished eating. If you want to take a break but have not yet finished, place your knife and fork by the side of your plate. A good waiter will not clear your plate from the table when you have finished eating. In the United States, it is considered rude to put your elbows on the table or to speak with your mouth full. It is also not polite to make a lot of noise when you eat; chewing noisily and slurping are bad manners in the United States.

r. Tip/Gratuity—It is customary to leave a tip of 15 percent of the bill at the end of the meal *unless* the bill says the gratuity is included (see further section on tipping).

s. Eating in public—In the United States, it is acceptable behavior to eat, drink, and chew gum in the street and on public transport. You should not eat in shops, banks, offices, or post offices.

t. Alcohol—It is illegal for young people under the age of twenty-one to consume alcohol. If you look younger than thirty you may be asked to provide photo ID in the form of a passport or driver's license. It is acceptable in American culture for men and women to drink as a form of social behavior.

b. *Working*

Looking for a job

There are many ways to look for a job in the United States. To increase your chances of finding a job, you can

- ask friends, neighbors, family, or others in your community about job openings or good places to work;

- look in the newspaper "classifieds" section under "employment";
- look for "help wanted" signs in the windows of local businesses;
- go to the employment or human resources offices of businesses in your area to ask about job openings;
- visit community agencies that help immigrants find jobs or job training programs;
- check bulletin boards in local libraries, grocery stores, and community centers for notices of job openings;
- check with the department of employment services for your state;
- search for jobs on the Internet. If you are using a computer at your library, the library staff can help you get started.

Applying for a job

Most employers will ask you to fill out a job application. This is a form with questions about your address, education, and past work experience. It may also ask for information about people you have worked with in the past. These are called references, and the employer may want to call them to ask questions about you.

You may need to create a résumé with a list of your work experience. A résumé tells your employer about your past jobs, your education or training, and your job skills. Take your résumé when you apply for work. A good résumé

- has your name, address, and phone number;
- lists your past jobs and includes dates you worked;
- shows your level of education;
- shows any special skills you have;
- is easy to read and has no mistakes.

Check with local community service agencies to see if they can help you write a résumé. Private businesses can help with this, too, but they charge a fee.

The job interview

Employers may want to meet with you to talk about the job. They will ask about your past work and your skills. You can practice answering questions about your past work and your skills with a friend or family member, so you will be ready. You can also ask questions of the employer. This is a good chance to find out about the job.

Employee benefits

In addition to your pay, some employers provide extra employment benefits. OBenefits may include

- medical care,
- dental care,
- eye care,
- life insurance,
- retirement plan.

Employers may pay some or all of the costs of these benefits. Ask about the benefits your employer will provide. You may also want to ask:

- What are the hours of work?
- How much does the job pay? (US law requires most employers to pay at least a "minimum wage," which is the lowest wage permitted.)
- How many vacation days are provided?
- How many sick days are provided?
- What benefits are included with the job?

During the interview, an employer can ask you many questions. However, employers are not allowed to ask some questions. No one should ask you about your race, color, sex, marriage, religion, country of origin, age, or any disability you may have.

Know your rights—federal laws protect employees

Several federal laws forbid employers from discriminating against people looking for a job. The United States has laws forbidding discrimination on grounds of

- race, color, religion, country of origin, and sex (Civil Rights Act);
- age (Age Discrimination in Employment Act);
- disabilities (Americans with Disabilities Act);
- sex (Equal Pay Act).

For more information about these protections, visit the US Equal Employment Opportunity Commission website at www.eeoc.gov or call (800) 669-4000 and (800) 669-6820 (for hearing impaired).

Other laws help keep workplaces safe, provide for leave in cases of family or medical emergencies, and provide temporary funds for unemployed workers. Visit the US Department of Labor website at www.dol.gov for more information about workers' rights.

What to expect when you are hired

When you go to your new job for the first time, you will be asked to fill out some forms. These include

- Form I-9: the Employment Eligibility Verification Form. By law, your employer must check to see that all newly hired workers are eligible to work in the United States. On your first day of work, you will need to fill in the I-9 form. Within three business days, you must show your employer your identity documents and work authorization documents. You can choose what documents to show as proof of your right to work in the United States, as long as the document is listed on the I-9 form. The list of acceptable documents is on the back of the I-9 form. Examples of acceptable documents are your Permanent Resident Card or an unrestricted Social Security number card in combination with a state-issued driver's license.
- Form W-4: the Employee's Withholding Allowance Certificate. Your employer should take federal taxes from your paycheck to send to the government. This is called "withholding tax." Form W-4 tells your employer to withhold taxes and helps you figure out the right amount to withhold.
- Other Forms: You may also need to fill out a tax withholding form for the state you live in and forms so that you can get benefits.

You may be paid each week, every two weeks, or once a month. Your paycheck will show the amount taken out for federal and state taxes, Social Security taxes, and any employment benefits you pay. Some employers will send your pay directly to your bank; this is called "direct deposit."

Speaking English at work

If you do not speak English, try to learn it as soon as possible through the free or low-cost English language classes in your community, often through the local public schools or community college. Knowing Erglish will help you in your job, your community, and your daily life.

Federal protection for immigrant workers

Federal law says that employers cannot discriminate against you because of your immigration status. Employers cannot

- refuse to hire you, or fire you, because of your immigration status or because you are not a US citizen;
- require you to show a permanent resident card or reject your lawful work papers;
- prefer hiring undocumented workers;
- discriminate against you because of your national origin (or country of origin);
- retaliate against any employee who complains of the above treatment.

For more information about your rights, or to file a complaint, call the Office of Special Counsel at (800) 255-7688 or (800) 237-2515 (for hearing impaired). If you do not speak English, interpreters are available to help you. You also can visit www.usdoj.gov/crt/osc for more information.

Drug tests and background checks

For some jobs, you may be required to take a test to make sure you are not using illegal drugs. Some jobs require that you have a background check, which is an investigation into your past activities and present circumstances.

The United States welcomes thousands of foreign workers in multiple occupations or employment categories every year. These include artists, researchers, cultural exchange participants, information technology specialists, religious workers, investors, scientists, athletes, nurses, agricultural workers, and others. All foreign workers must obtain permission to work legally in the United States. Each employment category for admission has different requirements, conditions, and authorized periods of stay. It is important that you adhere to the terms of your application or petition for admission and visa. Any violation can result in removal or denial of reentry into the United States.

Temporary (nonimmigrant) workers

A temporary worker is an individual seeking to enter the United States temporarily for a specific purpose. Nonimmigrants enter the United States for a temporary period of time, and once in the United States, are restricted to the activity or reason for which their nonimmigrant visa was issued.

Permanent (immigrant) workers

A permanent worker is an individual who is authorized to live and work permanently in the United States.

Students and exchange visitors

Students and exchange visitors may, under certain circumstances, be allowed to work in the United States. They must obtain permission from an authorized official at their school. The authorized official is known as a designated school official (DSO) for students and the responsible officer (RO) for exchange visitors.

Information for employers and employees

Employers must verify that an individual whom they plan to employ or continue to employ in the United States is authorized to accept employment in the United States. Individuals, such as those who have been admitted as permanent residents, granted asylum or refugee status, or admitted in work-related nonimmigrant classifications, may have employment authorization as a direct result of their immigration status. Other aliens may need to apply individually for employment authorization.

Temporary visitors for business

To visit the United States for business purposes, you will need to obtain a visa as a temporary visitor for business (B-1 visa), unless you qualify for admission without a visa under the Visa Waiver Program.

c. Transportation

There are many ways to travel in the United States. Many cities have buses, trains (also called subways), trolleys, or streetcars. Anyone can ride these vehicles for a small fee. In some places, you can buy a card good for several trips on subways or buses. You can also pay for each trip separately. Taxicabs, or taxis (or cabs), are cars that take you where you want to go for a fee. Taxis are more expensive than other types of public transportation.

d. Urban vs. rural lifestyle and major differences

How easily will you adjust to your new community and environment?

The United States is a very diverse country, offering a variety of climates, cultural heritage, and landscapes from coast to coast. Imagine yourself studying in the United States and think about the environment you want.

Virtually every US state includes settings that can range from urban (cities), suburban residential areas, or the rural countryside. US colleges and universities may be located in any one of these settings.

Which setting would be best for you?

Urban—Cities with larger populations providing convenient access to banking, stores, the arts, entertainment, public transportation, and international airports. Urban areas may have higher average living costs.

Suburban—Residential areas closer or farther from cities, with moderate population density and more spread-out restaurants and shopping areas. Suburban areas may have more moderate average living costs.

Rural—Countryside areas with smaller towns of fewer people and areas of land used for mining and agriculture. Rural areas may have lower average living costs.

e. *Getting a driver's license*

It is against the law to drive without a driver's license. You must apply for and get a driver's license if you want to drive. You get your driver's license from the state where you live.

f. *Vehicle ownership*

Owning a car can be a convenient way to get around. In the United States, you must also pay for car insurance, registering your vehicle, and licenses. Heavy traffic can make driving difficult in some cities. Think of all the costs and benefits before you decide to buy a car.

Ten tips for driving safely in the United States:

1. Drive on the right-hand side of the road.
2. Always have your driver's license and insurance card with you.
3. Always wear your seat belt.
4. Use proper seat belts and car safety seats for children.
5. Use your car's signals to show if you are turning left or right.
6. Obey all traffic laws and signals.
7. Pull over to the side of the road if an emergency vehicle—police car, fire truck, or ambulance—needs to pass you.
8. Do not pass a school bus when its red lights are flashing.

9. Do not drive if you have been drinking or taking drugs.
10. Be very careful when driving in fog, ice, rain, or snow.
11. A driver's license is used for identification in the United States. It is a good idea to get one, even if you do not own a car.

If you do not know how to drive, you can take driving lessons. Many public school districts have classes in driver education. You can also look under "Driving Instruction" in the yellow pages of the phone book.

TIP: Hitchhiking is not common in the United States. In many places it is illegal. For safety reasons, do not hitchhike and do not give rides to hitchhikers.

Short-term visitors

If you plan to drive when you visit the United States, check the driving rules in the state(s) you'll be visiting to verify that you can use your non-US driver's license. You should get an international driving permit (IDP), which translates the information contained on your official driver's license into ten languages.

The United States does not issue international driving permits to foreign visitors, so you will need to obtain this document in your home country before you travel to the United States.

Students

If you are a foreign student coming to the United States to study, you should contact the university or college you will be attending for information about driving.

Residents (non-US citizens)

The residency requirement for obtaining a US driver's license is different in each state.

If you are eligible to apply for a driver's license, you can only get a driver's license from the state where you live. Check with your state's department of motor vehicles to find out how to apply.

Once you receive your US driver's license from a state motor vehicle department, you can drive in all US states. Remember that the driving laws in each state differ, and it is your responsibility to know and obey the laws of the state where you are driving.

Check with the state office that issues driver's licenses to find out how to get one. These offices have different names in each state. Some common names are Department of Motor Vehicles (DMV), Department of Transportation, Motor Vehicle Administration, or Department of Public Safety. You can find these offices

in the blue pages of the phone book or get more information at www.usa.gov/
Topics/Motor_Vehicles.shtml

Some permanent residents already have a driver's license from another
country. You may be able to trade this for a license in your state. Check with your
state office to see if you can do this.

Importing a motor vehicle

Warning: Motor vehicles are subject to safety standards under the Motor
Vehicle Safety Act of 1966; revised under the Imported Vehicle Safety Compliance
Act of 1988; bumper standards under the Motor Vehicle Information and Cost
Savings Act of 1972, which became effective in 1978; and air pollution control
standards under the Clean Air Act of 1968, as amended in 1977 and 1990.

If vehicles manufactured abroad conform to US safety, bumper, and emission
standards, it is because these vehicles are exported for sale in the United States.
Therefore, it is unlikely that a vehicle obtained abroad meets all relevant standards.
Be skeptical of claims by a foreign dealer or other seller that a vehicle meets
these standards or can readily be brought into compliance. Vehicles entering the
United States that do not conform to US safety standards must be brought into
compliance, exported, or destroyed.

General information for persons entering the United States can be obtained at
a local CBP office, online at www.cbp.gov or by writing to:

US Customs and Border Protection
PO Box 7407
Washington, DC 20044

It is also possible to obtain copies from American embassies and consulates
abroad.

EPA has a detailed automotive fact manual describing emission requirements
for imported vehicles. You may obtain a copy of this manual, called the *Automotive
Imports Facts Manual*, or other information about importing motor vehicles, by
calling EPA's Imports Hotline at (734) 214-4100.

EPA's web page on Importing Vehicles and Engines contains additional
information (www.epa.gov).

You may reach DOT's vehicle hotline at (202) 366-5291 or communicate by fax
at (202) 366-1024.

The DOT website can provide further assistance (www.dot.gov).

Note: Importations from Afghanistan (Taliban), Cuba, Iran, Iraq, Libya, North
Korea, Sudan, Serbia/Montenegro/Kosovo, or Bosnia-Herzogovina that involve the

governments of those countries are generally prohibited pursuant to regulations issued by the Treasury Department's Office of Foreign Assets Control. Before attempting to make such an importation, information concerning the prohibitions and licensing policy should be obtained by contacting:

Director, Office of Foreign Assets Control
US Department of the Treasury
2nd Floor Annex
1500 Pennsylvania Avenue NW
Washington, DC 20220

You can call either (202) 622-2500 or (202) 622-2480, or fax (202) 622-1657, or visit the US Department of the Treasury's Office of Foreign Assets Control website: www.treasury.gov/about/organizational-structure/offices/Pages/Office-of-Foreign-Assets-Control.aspx

Documentation: For CBP clearance, you will need the shipper's or carrier's original bill of lading, the bill of sale, foreign registration, and any other documents covering the vehicle. You will also be required to complete EPA form 3520-1 and DOT form HS-7, declaring the emissions and safety provisions under which the vehicle is being imported. Vehicles that meet all US emission requirements will bear the manufacturer's label on the engine compartment, in English, attesting to that fact. For vehicles that lack such a label, the CBP inspector at the port of entry may require proof of eligibility to import under the EPA exemptions or exclusions specified on form 3520-1. Vehicles that do not meet all US emission requirements, unless eligible for exemption or exclusion, must be imported through an independent commercial importer (ICI). The EPA will not allow the vehicle's release to the owner until ICI work is complete. The ICI will perform any EPA-required modifications and be responsible for assuring that all EPA requirements have been met. Some vehicles cannot be successfully imported or modified by an ICI, however, and in general, ICI fees are very high.

Your car is not a shipping container. For your own safety, security, and convenience, do not use your car as a container for personal belongings. Your possessions are susceptible to theft while the vehicle is on the loading and unloading docks and in transit. Many shippers and carriers will not accept your vehicle if it contains personal belongings. The entire contents of your car must be declared to CBP on entry. Failure to do so can result in a fine or seizure of the car and its contents. Your vehicle may be subject to seizure, and you may incur a personal penalty, if anyone uses it as a conveyance of illegal narcotics.

As a returning US resident, you may apply for $800 CBP exemption and those of accompanying family members toward the value of the vehicle if it

- accompanies you on your return;
- is imported for personal use;
- was acquired during the journey from which you are returning.

For CBP purposes, a returning US resident is one who is returning from travel, work, or study abroad. After the exemption has been applied, a flat duty rate of 3 percent is applied toward the next $1,000 of the vehicle's value. The remaining amount is dutiable at the regular duty rate.

Free entry

Nonresidents may import a vehicle duty-free for personal use for up to (1) one year if the vehicle is imported in conjunction with the owner's arrival. Vehicles imported under this provision that do not conform to US safety and emission standards must be exported within one year and may not be sold in the United States. There is no exemption or extension of the export requirements.

Cars imported for other purposes

Nonresidents may import an automobile or motorcycle and its usual equipment free of duty for a temporary stay to take part in races or other specific purposes. However, prior written approval from the EPA is required, and such approval is granted only to those racing vehicles that EPA deems not capable of safe or practical use on streets and highways. If the contests are for other than money purposes, the vehicle may be admitted for ninety days without formal entry or bond if the CBP officer is satisfied as to the importer's identity and good faith. The vehicle becomes subject to forfeiture if it is not exported, or if a bond is not given within ninety days of its importation. Prior written approval must be obtained from DOT. A vehicle may be temporarily imported for testing, demonstration, or racing purposes. A vehicle may be permanently imported for show or display. Written approval from DOT is required and should be obtained before the vehicle is exported from the foreign country to the United States. Information on how to import a vehicle under show or display is available at DOT's NHTSA Vehicle Importation Regulations website. A vehicle permanently imported for show and display must comply with all US emission requirements as well and in general must be imported through an EPA-authorized ICI for modification and testing. EPA will not allow the vehicle to be released to its owner until ICI work is complete.

Federal tax

Certain imported automobiles may be subject to the gas-guzzler tax imposed by section 4064 of the Internal Revenue Code. An individual who imports an automobile for personal use, or a commercial importer, may be considered an importer for purposes of this tax and thus liable for payment of the tax.

The gas-guzzler tax is reported on Form 720, Quarterly Federal Excise Tax Return, and form 6197, Gas-Guzzler Tax. Additional information may be obtained from your local district office of the Internal Revenue Service.

Emission standards

Vehicles must be certified to US federal emission standards by their manufacturers for sale in the United States. Vehicles that do not meet these requirements are considered nonconforming. A currently certified ICI, a list of which is available from the EPA, must import nonconforming vehicles for you. The only EPA-authorized ICIs are located in the United States. It is therefore recommended that you contact an ICI to discuss costs for modification and testing before you decide to import a nonconforming vehicle. The ICI will be responsible for ensuring that your car complies with all US emission requirements. (As of July 1, 1998, EPA no longer has the one-time exemption for vehicles five or more model-years old.) Be aware that EPA will deny entry to certain makers, models, and model years if an ICI is not certified or is unwilling to accept responsibility for the vehicle(s) in question.

You may obtain additional information on emission control requirements or on ICIs from the US EPA Vehicle Programs and Compliance Division/Imports at (734) 214-4100, fax (734) 214-4676; or visit the website.

Individual state emission requirements may differ from those of the federal government.

Driver's plates and permits—Imported cars should bear the international registration marker. The international driving permit, issued in five languages, is a valuable asset. Consult an international automobile federation or your local automobile club about these documents.

US residents importing a new or used car should consult the Department of Motor Vehicles (DMV) in their state of residence about temporary license plates and what documentation their DMV would require from CBP.

Nationals of Central and South American countries that have ratified the Inter-American Convention of 1943 may drive their cars in the United States for touring purposes for one year or for the period of the validity of the documents, whichever is shorter, without US license plates or US driver's permits, provided the car carries the international registration marker and registration card, and the driver has the international driving permit.

Motorists visiting the United States as tourists from countries that have ratified the Convention on International Road Traffic of 1949 may drive in the United States for one year with their own national license plates (registration tags) and with their own personal driver's license.

Motorists from Canada and Mexico are permitted to tour in the United States without US license plates or US driver's permits under agreements between the United States and those countries.

Foreign nationals employed in the United States may use their foreign license tags from the port of entry to their destination in the United States.

g. *Crime and law enforcement*

Law enforcement in the United States

In the United States there are federal, state, and local law enforcement agencies that protect the public. In your community, law enforcement officers are the police or sheriff. Find out the phone number of the police station nearest you and keep it next to your telephone. Remember that police officers are there to protect you and your family from harm. Do not be afraid to report a crime, especially if you are the victim. Some criminals take advantage of immigrants because they think you will not report the crime to the police. If you are stopped by a police officer:

- Don't be afraid. Be polite and cooperative.
- Tell the officer if you do not speak English.
- If you are in a car, don't get out of the car until the officer tells you to.
- Keep your hands where the officer can see them.
- Don't reach into your pockets or into other areas of the car.

For emergency help, call 911. In the United States, you can call 911 on any telephone to get emergency help. Call 911 to

- report a fire;
- report a crime in progress;
- call an ambulance for emergency medical help;
- report suspicious activities, such as screams, calls for help, or gunshots.

Calls to 911 are usually answered within twelve seconds. You may be put on hold. Do not hang up! When the operator answers, there will be silence on the phone for several seconds. Do not hang up. Wait for the operator to speak.

If you do not speak English, tell the operator what language you speak. An interpreter should come on the line.

The 911 operator will ask you questions to find out what and where the emergency is. Keep calm and answer these questions. Try to stay on the phone with the operator until you answer all questions.

When not to call 911

Call 911 for serious, life-threatening emergencies only. Calling 911 for the wrong reason may keep someone else from getting the help they need. Do not call 911 to

- ask for directions;
- ask for information about public services;
- find out if someone is in jail;
- report situations that are not emergencies;
- ask for information about animal control;
- talk to a police officer about something that is not an emergency.

If you have a question for the police, call the nonemergency number for the police department listed in the blue pages of your phone book.

h. *Personal security*

Keeping your home and family safe

Get ready before emergencies happen. Here are some things you can do to be safe: Be sure your doors have good locks and keep them locked at all times. Don't give your door keys to strangers. Be careful about opening your door to strangers. Before you open the door, ask who they are and what they want.

Smoke alarms make a loud noise when there is smoke in your house or apartment. Make sure you have smoke alarms on the ceiling near bedrooms and on each floor of your house. Replace the batteries in your smoke alarm twice a year. Check the alarm once each month to make sure it works.

Find out where the nearest hospital and police and fire stations are located. Keep these important phone numbers (police station, fire department, and doctor) near your phone, where you can easily find them.

Find the main valves for gas, electricity, and water in your home. Be sure you know how to turn them off by hand.

Prepare a disaster kit that includes a flashlight, portable radio, extra batteries, blankets, a first-aid kit, and enough canned or packaged food and bottled water to last for three days. Also include trash bags, toilet paper, and pet food, if needed. Keep all these things in one place that is easy to find.

Practice with your family how to get out of your house in case of a fire or other emergency.

Ask about emergency plans at your children's school. Be sure your child knows what to do. Ask where you can go to meet your child in an emergency.

What you can do

To help keep your neighborhood safe, get to know your neighbors. Talk with them about how to handle an emergency in your area. If you have neighbors with disabilities, see if they need special help.

Many neighborhoods have a neighborhood watch. The neighborhood watch is a group of people from the neighborhood. They take turns walking the streets at night to discourage criminal activity. If there is a neighborhood watch in your area, you can volunteer to participate. If you want to get a neighborhood watch started, call your local police department for help.

Visit www.usaonwatch.org for more information.

When you help others to be safe, you help your community and nation. You can get more involved in your community through your local Citizen Corps Council.

Visit www.citizencorps.gov for more information.

First aid

Learn how to help in certain emergency situations, such as when someone is bleeding or choking. This is called "first aid." You can take a first aid training class through your local Red Cross. Call your local Red Cross office or the National Safety Council to ask about classes in your area. Find more information at www. redcross.org or www.nsc.org

Keep a first aid kit at home, at work, and in your car. A first aid kit has items you can use for small injuries or for pain, such as bandages, antiseptic wipes, pain medicine, instant ice packs, and gloves. You can buy a good first aid kit at your local drugstore. (800) 222-1222.

Poison control

Many things in your home can be poisonous if they are swallowed. These can include cleaning products, medicine, paint, alcohol, cosmetics, and even some plants. Keep these things away from young children.

If someone swallows a poisonous substance, call the Poison Control Center right away at (800) 222-1222. You can get help twenty-four hours a day, seven days a week. Have the poisonous substance with you when you call. Tell the operator what it is. If you do not speak English, tell the operator so an interpreter can help you. Calls to the Poison Control Center are confidential and free.

i. *Import-export regulations: free import*

Residents

Exemption of USD 200 worth of dutiable items—For residents that travelled abroad more than once in a thirty-day period or who have been out of the country for at least forty-eight hours. If the worth of the items brought in exceeds the above USD 200, then the whole amount is dutiable. You may include with the $200 exemption your choice of the following:

- fifty cigarettes, and
- ten cigars, and
- 150 mL (5 fl. oz.) of alcoholic beverages, or
- 150 mL (5 fl. oz.) of perfume containing alcohol

Exemption of USD 800 worth of dutiable items—For residents who have been out of the country at least forty-eight hours and their duty-free exemption was not used in the preceding thirty days. The duty-free allowances may include the following maximum quantities:

- tobacco products: two hundred cigarettes and one hundred cigars
- for persons of twenty-one years or older, 1 L of alcohol
- other goods for personal use

Exemption of USD 1,600 worth of dutiable items—For US residents who are traveling from US insular possessions (US Virgin Islands, American Samoa, or Guam) or for residents who are coming back from US insular possessions, the countries of the Caribbean Basin, or Andean countries.

The exemption constitutes the following:

USD 1,600 worth of items originated only from the US insular countries or in the instance of travel to US insular possessions and to the Caribbean Basin or Andean countries, the worth of articles can amount to USD 1,600, but the worth of the articles originated in the latter cannot exceed USD 800, otherwise a duty must be paid.

The tobacco allowance for the USD 1,600 exemption is up to one thousand cigarettes, but only two hundred can be of the Caribbean Basin or Andean origin (as all allowance for duty free tobacco coming from foreign countries cannot exceed two hundred.)

The alcohol allowance as a part of the USD 1,600 exemption can constitute up to five liters, but only four liters can be of the Caribbean Basin or Andean origin.

Nonresidents

- tobacco products: two hundred cigarettes and one hundred cigars
- one liter of alcohol for persons of twenty-one years or older
- other goods for personal use
- USD 100 worth of dutiable items as a gift

Nonresidents are allowed up to $100 worth of merchandise. To claim this exemption, you must remain in the United States for at least seventy-two hours, and the gifts must accompany you.

This $100 gift exemption can be claimed only once every six months. You may include one hundred cigars within the gift exemption, but alcoholic beverages may not be included. Family members may not group their gift exemptions. If you've used your gift exemption and then return to the United States before the six-month period has ended, you may still bring in up to $200 worth of merchandise free of duty for your personal use. Any of the following may be included in this $200 exemption:

- fifty cigarettes
- one hundred cigars (non-Cuban)
- 150 mL of alcoholic beverages
- 150 mL of perfume containing alcohol, or equivalent amounts of each

If you exceed any of these limitations, however, or if the total value of all dutiable articles exceeds $200, no exemption can be applied.

Applicable for residents of the United States and nonresidents:
Prohibited

- food or any products thereof (dried, canned, etc.);
- narcotics and some medication containing prohibited substances;
- absinthe (unless thujone free);
- plants, seeds, vegetables, fruits;
- soil, livestock, or animal pests;
- biological (bacteria cultures, fungi specimens, viruses, and others for research, etc., permissible only with APHIS permit);
- unprepared fish and fish eggs;
- imports from embargoed countries (Iran, Cuba, Myanmar, and Sudan) and leather souvenirs imported from Haiti (e.g., drums);
- endangered wildlife species and products thereof (for example clothing and accessories);
- cultural artifacts from Byzantine period, pre-Columbian period, Khmer sculptures, etc. (unless with permission);
- dog and cat fur;
- items infringing trade and copyright regulations;
- fully automatic weapons and semiautomatic weapons (see the restricted section);
- pornography;
- articles infringing copyrights;
- traitorous material and material igniting agitation;
- hazardous articles like fireworks, uncertified toys, health hazardous substances.

Restricted

- Cats and dogs must be accompanied by
  - a health certificate, issued within thirty days at point of origin. The certificate must state that animals have lived in an area that has not been under quarantine due to contagious, infectious, or transmissible disease;
  - a rabies certificate issued within six months (if the animal is over four months old).
- Birds require a health certificate issued immediately prior to shipment. The certificate must state that the birds were found free of psittacosis

or ornithosis. For more detailed information please contact US Fish and Wildlife Service.

- Please contact the US Fish and Wildlife Service about seafood.
- All health-related drugs need to be properly labeled (preferably in their original packaging), and the quantity should not be in excess of the amount you would normally need for the duration of your stay. It is strongly advisable to accompany the drugs with prescription or written letter from your personal physician.
- Arms and ammunition are restricted (nonresidents only).

In order to import firearms, ammunition, and implements of war, an approved ATF Form 6-Part I is required. ATF Form 6 should be submitted approximately sixty days prior to the intended importation ("Application and Permit for Importation of Firearms, Ammunition and Implements of War").

Free Export

- No restrictions on tobacco, alcohol, or any other allowed items
- Prohibited:
    - narcotics and some medication containing prohibited substances;
    - absinthe (or other alcohols containing Artemisia absinthium);
    - biological material (bacteria cultures, fungi specimens, viruses, and others for research, etc., permissible only with APHIS permit);
    - endangered species that have not been outlined by CITES convention (to make sure that your item is allowed, contact the Fish and Wildlife Service);
    - items infringing trade and copyright regulations.
- Restricted (dependent on declaring):
    - Cultural artifacts (e.g., Byzantine period, Pre-Columbian period, Khmer sculptures, etc.) must be accompanied by permission.
    - Endangered animals and plants and products thereof as outlined by the CITES convention will require permit from CITES.
- It is advisable that all valuable articles produced outside United States be registered by a customs inspector before leaving the United States.

j. *Death and funerals*

Death

In the event that someone dies in a hospital or medical care facility, the death must be pronounced by someone with the authority to do so (such as a doctor or hospice nurse). This person will certify the cause, time, and place of death. This legal form is necessary for many reasons, including life insurance, property, and financial issues.

The doctor may ask you if you would like an autopsy. This is a medical procedure conducted by a specially trained physician to learn more about what caused death.

After the death, how long you can stay with the body may depend on where death happens. If your religious, ethnic, or cultural background requires any customs soon after death, make sure to notify authorities or attending doctors so that you can observe them.

If the body is transported to the medical examiner or coroner's office, then arrangements should be made with a funeral home to pick up the body. If the death occurs in a hospital or medical facility, then they may call the funeral home for you.

Funerals

In the United States, funeral customs can vary widely between religious and cultural affiliations. In general, most funerals follow a similar pattern: visitation, funeral, and burial service, which will be described in more detail below.

The visitation is when the body of the deceased person is placed on display for family and friends to visit. The viewing is either open or closed casket. In an open casket the body is visible; in a closed casket the body is not visible. This generally occurs one to two nights before the funeral.

This step is sometimes not observed by certain cultural groups and religions (as is the case in Jewish funerals).

The funeral is a memorial service, which is generally officiated by clergy. Funerals might take place at a church, a funeral home, or even someone's home. Funeral services include religious rites, words of comfort by the clergy or person officiating the event, and in many cases a eulogy, which is a speech that discusses memories of the person who passed away. These are usually made by someone with a close relationship to the person or family.

The burial service is conducted at the site of the grave or tomb. This is the point in the proceedings where the person is buried or cremated. In most cases, the burial service will immediately follow the funeral, and in this case, the attendees of the funeral will travel in a procession to the burial site.

Your religion or culture may proscribe different funeral arrangements or traditions. Discuss these with the funeral home to ensure that these are observed to the extent possible. There are many different funeral traditions and arrangements in the United States, so do not feel limited by what is "normal" or "typical" when remembering your loved ones.

k. *Etiquette and behavior*

Meeting

When people meet for the first time, they generally shake hands and introduce themselves and the people whom they are with. When doing this, make eye contact and smile. Handshakes are firm and brief, and they should be made confidently. This may be done between men and women.

In most social situations people will begin by calling each other by their first names. If you are not certain that this is appropriate, you can use Mr., Mrs., Ms., etc., until you are invited to move to a first-name basis.

Americans are very direct in their communication and expect you to be as well.

Dining

Americans socialize over meals and drinks quite frequently. If you are invited to a dinner it is important to be on time (ten minutes ahead if a small gathering, thirty minutes if a larger one). Table manners are more relaxed in the United States than in many countries, but it is important to be aware that there are some basic rules, which are listed below:

- If you wish to bring another guest always check with your host first.
- Place your napkin on your lap as soon as you sit down. You may use it to wipe your hands and your mouth, but it should return to your lap until you are finished with your meal.
- The fork is held in the right hand and is used for eating. The knife is used for cutting or spreading food.
- You can rest the fork or the knife on the plate between mouthfuls. Once you have finished eating, you can place them side by side in the center of the plate.
- Do not begin eating until everyone is at the table, and the host or hostess has begun.
- Do not rest your elbows on the table.
- You can decline any type of food or drink without much explanation.
- Do not talk with your mouth full.
- Some foods are eaten by hand. When in doubt, just watch your surroundings or ask someone.

- When you need to leave the table to use the bathroom, it is polite to ask to be excused to do so.
- Always thank your host for inviting you and for the meal.

Business. Business cards are exchanged in the United States, but this is done without any formal ritual or procedure. Cards may be exchanged with one hand or two and may be kept on the table or even put immediately into the recipient's pocket.

In the United States, it is considered very important to be on time for meetings. If you are going to be late, it is expected that you will call ahead and let the person that you are meeting know that you will be late. If you will be very late (more than thirty minutes) then it is likely that the meeting may be rescheduled to a later point in time. Americans usually fill up their business calendar with calls and appointments and are less flexible in scheduling meetings and calls than in other countries. It is also important in many settings to schedule a meeting in advance, because in most professions (aside from retail) it is not usually considered polite to arrive without an appointment.

Business meetings may appear to be casual, but they are taken seriously and are usually focused on some sort of objective. This objective may be discussed with you, or it may not be. There will be little time spent on personal discussions or "small talk" in meetings, and it is acceptable to start discussing the business issue at hand right away. Business issues will be discussed directly and openly. Americans value their time, and therefore, place little emphasis on subtlety in business. It will be expected that you are direct and "get to the point" in short order.

Most meetings will have an objective, and at the end of the meeting the participants will discuss what to do next. It is generally the objective of a business meeting to have an oral agreement prior to the end of the meeting, with further agreement to sign a contract. After the contract is signed, then a relationship may be developed, but not in all cases. American businesspeople are highly focused on efficiency and getting to an agreement quickly rather than truly understanding all of the parties' objectives in the matter.

Americans also do not always insist on meeting people that they are doing business with, and much business is conducted over the telephone. It is not uncommon for Americans to have clients or business associates of many years that they have never met.

I. *Shopping*

Shopping is major economic and social activity in the United States. The shopping experience is as varied as the geography. In major cities there are many shops and malls inside of the cities; in smaller cities most of the shopping venues (called shopping or strip malls) are located in the suburbs. Most shopping in the United States occurs in local stores, shopping malls, discount stores, department stores, outlet malls, and online.

Local stores. Shopping at local stores can be a different experience depending on where you are shopping. You can find local stores that sell specialized items such as clothing, hardware and tools, paper goods, toys, handicrafts that may be unique to a geographical area, antiques, art, and many other items. Shopping in local stores can be a unique experience, as the merchandise selection is made by the owner.

Shopping malls. Shopping malls are usually located outside of the city. Most shopping malls have a variety of stores and places to eat, and they may have other activities, such as movies or children's playgrounds. In the United States, you may find that many shopping malls have similar stores and normally contain at least one major store or department store.

Discount stores. Discount stores are places that sell affordably priced merchandise. These are generally larger stores and may have a variety of merchandise, such as clothing, health-care items, kitchen and household necessities, and sporting goods.

Department stores. Department stores are generally large stores (multiple floors) with a wide selection of clothing and merchandise. Quality is generally higher in department stores, and it is here that you might find the latest brands and other fashionable clothing. These stores are generally part of national chains. This means that you can find similar merchandise in different locations.

Outlet malls. Outlet malls are generally located outside of major cities and are a collection of higher-end stores that sell their previous season or slightly irregular merchandise at lower prices than in their primary stores. Merchandise sold here is generally sold at 20–40 percent below department store prices.

A note on sales taxes

There is no value added federal tax in the United States; however, most states and cities levy a sales tax that is generally 4–8 percent. In almost all cases, these taxes are not included in the price, so remember that you will need to add this to the cost when you are making a purchase decision.

m. *Fashion and dress*

Dress in the United States is generally more casual than many parts of the world, with the exception of professional business attire. Fashion is very diverse and highly influenced by the local culture, weather, geography, venue, and socioeconomic level. What may be seen as normal in one location may or may not be seen in the same way in another. For example, in Hawaii people wear Hawaiian shirts to business meetings; this would not be acceptable in a business meeting in New York City. Executives tend to dress formally in most parts of the country.

Dress norms in the United States are generally consistent with other postindustrial Western nations. The western states are usually known for being more informal than those states located in the East. When you are meeting someone for the first time (especially for business), it is best to dress conservatively (men should wear a business suit unless you are sure that the parties that you are meeting are very casual), and women can wear a business suit, dress, or pantsuit.

If you are in doubt about what to wear to an event, business meeting, or job interview, just ask someone. Most people who have been in the United States for a few years have a general idea of what may be seen as appropriate and will happily provide you some advice.

n. *Culture Shock*

Culture shock for new immigrants (or anyone living in a foreign environment) is very real, and it is highly likely that you will experience some form of it. Generally speaking, culture shock is created by a mismatch of cultural attitudes. This term was first introduced in 1958 to describe the anxiety produced when someone moves to a new environment that that may have a different language, customs, and food, and when it is difficult to determine what type of behavior is appropriate in a certain circumstance. This difficulty can be on a business, social, legal, or cultural level, and it is experienced by students, businesspeople, retirees, and visitors alike.

While almost everyone who moves to a new environment will experience some form of culture shock, not everyone experiences all of the symptoms to the same extent. Its effects vary by individual. Symptoms of culture shock can be any of the following:

- anger, irritability, resentment
- inability or desire to interact with others

- anxiety
- trouble sleeping (insomnia)
- a desire to sleep too much
- sadness, feeling of isolation, melancholy and lack of desire to meet new people
- feeling resentful to your new environment
- reluctance to speak English
- lack of confidence
- inability to solve simple problems
- feelings of loss of identity
- idealizing your original country or culture or feeling excessively homesick
- feeling lost
- feelings of hostility, such as being abused, overlooked, or exploited

There are some distinct stages of culture shock that studies have shown are especially common to everyone who lives abroad.

The initial stage (euphoria or "honeymoon stage")

During the first few weeks of living in the new environment, most people are excited about their new country, eager to learn the new culture and environment, and full of energy. Once this excitement wears off, and the person must adjust to the normal difficulties of life, the second stage begins.

Irritability

During this stage, you might encounter the frustrations of trying to live in your new home, dealing with a foreign culture that may not make sense to you, and navigating through daily life. You may experience difficulties in being understood (not only in just a language context, but this may also be in business or negotiation) during this phase. This difficulty can result in feelings of isolation, anger, impatience, discontent, and feeling incompetent. This is happening because you are adjusting to your new environment and a new culture. This adjustment takes time to complete.

Adjustment

After some time, patience, and understanding, you will start to become more used to the new culture and will gradually adjust without constant anxiety. In most cases, you will not even notice that this is happening, and it will not be until you realize that you are able to interpret cultural clues that you are beginning to adjust.

Adaptation

You will eventually adjust to your new culture and will be able to function, understanding the complex cultural environment with more ease. The culture will become more and more familiar to you, and eventually you may feel a part of it.

Dealing with culture shock

While you may not be able to prevent the effect of culture shock, there are some things that you can do in order to minimize the effects and the speed at which you might be able to adjust.

- Keep an open mind and stay positive. This is a key component to adjusting to a new environment. People in the United States may do and say things very differently from your home country, but they are not strange or unapproachable. Most Americans like to talk, laugh, and help. If you are having trouble expressing yourself, just tell the person whom you are talking to that you are working on your English and that you need some extra time to explain yourself; most people will be understanding and supportive.

- Try to speak English as much as possible. Believe it or not, by improving your English, you will improve not only your cultural understanding but also your ability to communicate your needs and intentions to other people. You may feel uncomfortable at first, but you will become better with time and practice, and this will help your adjustment.

- Take care of your health. It is very important to get plenty of sleep, get some physical exercise (if you are able), and eat healthful meals. Feeling good will help you approach the situation from a more positive perspective.

Note: If you are having severe symptoms or are feeling hopeless or depressed, speak to a counselor, doctor, or health-care professional.

o. *Taking care of your money*

Banking and payments
Getting a bank account

A bank account is a safe place to keep your money. Banks have different kinds of accounts. Checking accounts (for paying bills) and savings accounts (for earning interest on your money) are two common ones. You can open an account for yourself or a joint account with your spouse or another person. Banks may charge you fees for some of their services.

Credit unions and savings and loan associations are other choices for banking. Your employer may have a credit union that you can join. Credit unions provide most of the same services as banks, but many offer extra services. Compare the services, fees, hours, and locations of banks before you open an account, so you can choose one that best meets your needs.

TIP: Many stores offer check-cashing services and overseas money-wiring services, but these cost money. Check to see if your bank offers these services at a lower cost. When you open a bank account, you will be asked to prove your identity. You can use your permanent resident card or driver's license. You will also need to give the bank some money—called a deposit—to put into your new account. After a few days, you can take money out of your account. This is called withdrawing money. You can withdraw money by writing a check, going to an automatic teller machine (ATM), or filling out a withdrawal form in the bank.

It is not safe to leave large amounts of money in your house. It is also not safe to carry around large amounts of cash. It could be stolen or lost. Your money is protected if you put it in a bank that is a member of the Federal Deposit Insurance Corporation (FDIC). The FDIC provides banks with insurance to protect your money. If your bank closes, the FDIC will pay you the amount of the money in your account up to $100,000. Make sure the bank you choose has FDIC insurance.

Using your bank account

You can get money from your bank account using a personal check or ATM card. Be sure that only you and, if you have one, your joint account holder have access to your account.

Personal checks

You will get a supply of personal checks when you open your checking account. These checks are forms that you fill out to pay for something. Checks tell your bank to pay the person or business you have written on the check. Keep these checks in a safe place.

ATM cards

You can ask your bank for an ATM card. This is a small plastic card linked to your bank account. Use this card to get cash or deposit money in your account at an ATM machine. Usually you do not pay a fee for using your own bank's ATM. You may pay a fee if you use an ATM owned by another bank.

Debit cards

Your bank may give you a debit card to use for your checking account. Sometimes your ATM card can also be used as a debit card. Debit cards allow you to pay for something without writing a check by having your bank send the money directly to the business you are buying from.

Bank checks

Bank checks are checks that the bank makes out at your request. You give the bank money, and they make out a bank check for that amount of money to the person or business you want to send it to.

Credit cards

Credit cards—also called charge cards—allow you to make purchases and pay for them later. Banks, stores, and gas stations are some businesses that can give you a credit card. You get a bill in the mail each month for purchases you have made with your credit card.

Your credit rating

In the United States, the way you handle your credit is very important. There are organizations that create a credit score or credit rating for you, depending on how you pay bills, how many loans you take out, if you are on time with your payments, and other factors. This credit rating is very important when you want to buy a home or car or take out a loan. Here are some things you can do to get a good credit rating:

- Pay all your bills on time.
- Keep your credit card balances low. Pay at least the minimum amount due each month.
- Don't apply for a lot of loans or credit cards.

Under federal law, you can get one free credit report once a year. If you would like to get a copy of your credit rating report, you can call (877) 322-8228 or go to www.annualcreditreport.com.

Money Transfers
Money transfers in the United States

Money transfers in the United States are generally simple and require a form of official identification. If you have a bank account, you can generally make electronic transfers to other people's accounts in the United States with relative ease. You can also use wire services such as Western Union, MoneyGram, or PayPal, an online payment system that allows you to transfer money both inside and outside of the United States. There will be certain information that you will need to provide to the bank or money transfer service about yourself and the recipient; if you are unsure, ask them for this information so that you can provide it.

Keep in mind that it is very difficult, if not impossible, to obtain a return of your money once it is transferred electronically. Therefore, if you are making a transfer to pay for goods or services, it may be better to use a credit card with fraud protection than a wire service. This is even more important if you are transferring a large amount of money. If you intend to use a money transfer service to make a large purchase, such as a car or a house, it would be wise to obtain professional advice (from a lawyer, for example) before doing this. There are generally acceptable ways of making large purchases that include the use of escrow agents (third parties who hold the money until the legal agreements have been signed and filed by the parties) for the safety of both parties. If you are unsure of whether or not this is applicable, talk to a professional. Do not send large amounts of money to someone whom you do not know. Wire fraud is a serious problem in most countries, and the United States is no exception to this, so be especially vigilant when someone asks you to send money electronically.

It is also generally more expensive to use third-party transfer services than your bank, so shop carefully.

Money transfers outside of the United States (international money transfers)

Money transfers to locations outside of the United States are highly regulated and generally require a higher level of scrutiny of both the sender of the funds and also the financial institutions that make the transactions possible. In general, wire transfers to relatives and other overseas are not a problem, but you must be mindful of the above few issues.

Money transfers and taxes

In the event that you transfer, in the form of a gift, more than $14,000 to any recipient (per person) in any year, you must file a gift tax return. Second, there are specific prohibitions against sending funds to certain countries, to certain individuals, and through certain prohibited financial institutions due to economic sanctions by the US government. Failure to abide by these prohibitions can have harsh civil and criminal penalties.

The Office of Foreign Assets Control (OFAC) of the US Department of the Treasury administers and enforces economic and trade sanctions based on US foreign policy and national security goals against targeted foreign countries and regimes, terrorists, international narcotics traffickers, those engaged in activities related to the proliferation of weapons of mass destruction, and other threats to the national security, foreign policy, or economy of the United States. OFAC acts under presidential national emergency powers, as well as authority granted by specific legislation, to impose controls on transactions and freeze assets under US jurisdiction. Many of the sanctions are based on United Nations and other international mandates, are multilateral in scope, and involve close cooperation with allied governments.

Prohibited transactions are trade or financial transactions and other dealings in which US persons may not engage unless authorized by OFAC or are expressly exempted by statute. Because each program is based on different foreign policy and national security goals, prohibitions may vary between programs.

OFAC administers a number of US economic sanctions and embargoes that target geographic regions and governments. Comprehensive sanctions programs include Burma (Myanmar), Cuba, Iran, Sudan, and Syria. Other partial programs include the Western Balkans, Belarus, Cote d'Ivoire, Democratic Republic of the Congo, Iraq, Liberia (former regime of Charles Taylor), Persons Undermining the Sovereignty of Lebanon or Its Democratic Processes and Institutions, Libya, North Korea, Somalia, and Zimbabwe, as well as other programs targeting individuals and entities located around the world. Those programs currently relate to foreign narcotics traffickers, foreign terrorists, transnational criminal organizations, and WMD proliferators.

It is important to note that in programs that are not comprehensive, there are no broad prohibitions on dealings with countries, but only against specific, named individuals and entities. The names are incorporated into OFAC's list of Specially Designated Nationals and Blocked Persons (SDN List) which includes over six thousand names of companies and individuals who are connected with the sanctions targets. A number of the named individuals and entities are known to move from country to country and may end up in locations where they would be least expected. US persons are prohibited from dealing with SDNs wherever they are located, and all SDN assets are blocked. Entities that a person on the SDN List owns (defined as a direct- or indirect-ownership interest of 50 percent or more) are also blocked, regardless of whether that entity is separately named on the SDN List. Because OFAC's programs are dynamic and constantly changing, it is very important to check OFAC's website on a regular basis to ensure that your SDN List is current and that you have complete information regarding current restrictions affecting countries and parties with which you plan to do business.

Specific attention should be paid when sending funds to countries such as Iran, North Korea, Syria, Zimbabwe, Burma, the Balkans, and Cuba. Additionally, it is wise before sending funds to someone that you don't know in a foreign country to check them against the SDN List. You can learn more about OFAC and specific prohibitions on their website:

www.treasury.gov/resource-center/sanctions/Pages/default.aspx

p. *Tipping*

Be prepared to tip in US restaurants (somewhere that takes your order at the table and brings you the food) where the generally expected tip is 15–20 percent (of the total bill before taxes), depending on the level of service. You cannot be forced to pay a tip by legal means, unless the charge is clearly marked prior to service, which can include gratuities (tips).

In fast-food restaurants, restaurants where you order at a counter, and coffee shops that do not have table service, a tip is not expected. In some cases you will see a "tip jar" at the counter in these places. It is a matter of confusion, even to longtime residents of the United States, whether this type of tip is expected or necessary. You may choose in this case to tip or not.

Other types of tips and amounts deemed generally acceptable are listed below:

- bartenders: $1–2 per drink or 15–20 percent of the total bill
- buffet restaurants: generally 5 percent of the total (if any table service)
- restaurant servers: 15–25 percent depending on service (if service is very bad, 10 percent; if terrible notify the manager)
- bellman/porter at a hotel: $1–2 per bag
- taxi driver: 10–15 percent of the fare
- valet parking attendant: $2–5 per car, when picking up
- hairdresser: 10–20 percent of the total
- tour guides: 15–20 percent depending on service level
- hotel housekeeping: $2–3 per night, $4–5 in high-end hotels

q. *Gift Giving*

There is no clear expectation of gift giving in US culture, especially in business. While gifts may be appreciated, they are generally not expected. Families generally observe their own cultural or religious traditions as it applies to gift giving inside the family, and these expectations generally do not extend to third parties. Very expensive gifts given outside of the family are uncommon and may be met with uncertainty.

Gifts in the business environment

Gifts (if given at all) are generally given after the business transaction, not before. In some cases the giving of gifts may violate corporate policies and even laws, so be certain of these before considering gifts. If you do give business gifts, then something that has a relevance to the project would be recommended. In most situations, gifts are opened and shown to all present at the time that they are received.

During the holiday season, gifts may be exchanged between coworkers and business associates. It is important that you do not choose gifts with religious connotations unless you are certain of the religious background of the person receiving the gift. It is also important that you do not give gifts in a business setting that may be considered too personal or have any sexual connotations (such as perfume or clothing to women if you are a man).

Social gifts

Social gifts are not generally expected except in a few circumstances. If you are invited to dinner at someone's house, you may bring a small gift; something to be consumed at the dinner (a bottle of wine, chocolates) or flowers would be appropriate. If you stay in someone's house for a few days, then a small gift or thank-you note is welcome. Taking someone out to a meal is probably the most popular form of gift giving, but make sure that the context is appropriate. An example is inviting a person who is married out to dinner without his or her spouse, which may be viewed as inappropriate. When giving gifts to children, take into account the values or desires of the parents.

r. *Business dress*

Business dress in the United States depends on industry, location, and climate. In most cases business is informal and does not require wearing a suit (for men, or a formal dress for women) unless the setting is professional, legal, or associated with the financial services. If you are giving a presentation or attending a job interview, it is better to be overdressed (more formally dressed than required) than underdressed.

The United States has a concept that is called "business casual," which the majority of workplaces adhere to. It means professional pants (or a skirt for a woman) and a more casual shirt, but it does not include T-shirts, athletic wear, or beach attire.

If you are unsure of what to wear to a meeting, just ask the organizer or someone else attending. They should be able to help you.

s. *Names*

Names in the United States are usually written with the first (or given) name first and the last name second. The first letters of each name are capitalized. In some cases people may also include their middle name.

If the conversation or communication is more formal, or you have not met the person to whom you are addressing, it is appropriate to address them as Mr., Mrs., or Ms. (unless they are a professional, and in this case you would use Dr., Prof., etc. in the form of address). This form of address is generally only for people who are considered adults. If you are uncertain whether or not a woman is married, it is appropriate to address her as Ms. until you learn otherwise.

Because of the informality in the United States, it is also common for people to address each other by their first names, even if they do not know each other, or there is a difference in age.

Because the United States is comprised of many different people from many places, it is possible that names may take different forms. When in doubt, ask someone from the region what is appropriate, or take a more formal approach; this is rarely offensive.

t. *Negotiating*

Negotiating for things or business in the United States may be foreign to you. In part this is because the United States does not have a homogenous culture, and the forms of negotiation may be very different, depending on where they are taking place.

There are some more general concepts that are more or less universal in US negotiations:

Time is money. Time is a commodity to most people in the United States. Time is "saved" and "spent" just like money. Because time has a perceived value, you may be surprised that business in the United States happens much faster, and the length of negotiations is much shorter than in many places. US businesspeople feel less need to completely understand their counterparties, and therefore, you might be surprised when they move right to business within a short time after the start of a business meeting or spend a very short time discussing issues and are quick to make decisions.

US businesspeople generally prefer to begin meetings on time, with prompt beginnings and endings; rely on specific, detailed, and explicit communications; and prefer to talk in a clear sequence. Because time is money, many people view lateness as evidence of lack of respect.

Win-win negotiations

US businesspeople are looking for mutually beneficial relationships (there are always exceptions to this) and generally are not looking to take all of the advantage from a business position. Most negotiations take place from the perspective of what is perceived as fair and equitable (although this position varies across cultures and industry). The ultimate objective of most business negotiations is a win-win where both parties benefit.

Agreement is usually considered final

Once the agreement has been made and is signed, it is generally considered final. If you attempt to renegotiate the terms or change the agreement after it has been signed, this will be met with considerable resistance, and in some cases, anger or resentment. Honesty in business dealings is seen as an important feature of doing business in the United States.

u. *Socializing (making connections)*

People in the United States are generally open and friendly and more direct than in many countries. While this may be difficult to get used to at first, it makes it relatively easy to make friends and new connections. It is not uncommon to meet people in the ordinary course of your day, as people may talk to you as you are in line, on the bus, or doing just about anything.

Many people are surprised at the ease with which Americans may converse with people whom they do not know, and it is not uncommon for people to ask personal questions to complete strangers. This is merely an American form of conversation and should not be taken with offense.

Americans also make eye contact and generally shake hands when meeting. They generally continue to make eye contact throughout the conversation.

If you are hoping to make new friends and meet people, public places like schools, community centers, and churches and other religious institutions are good places to do this. Many Americans are concerned about their personal safety and like to meet new people in public places.

v. *Sports and fitness*

Sports

Sports play an important role in American society. They enjoy tremendous popularity, but more important, they are vehicles for transmitting such values as fair play, team work, integrity, and hard work. Sports have contributed to racial and social integration and over history have been a "social glue" bonding the country together.

The United States offers almost limitless opportunities to engage in sports—either as a participant or as a spectator. Team sports have been part of life in North America since the colonies were established. Native American peoples played a variety of ball games, including some that may be viewed as an earlier form of lacrosse. The typical American sports of baseball, basketball, and football, however, arose from games that were brought to America by the first settlers who arrived from Europe in the seventeenth century. These games were refashioned and elaborated in the course of the nineteenth century.

Various social rituals have grown up around athletic contests. The local high-school football or basketball game represents the biggest event of the week for residents in many communities across the United States. Fans of major university and professional football teams often gather in parking lots outside stadiums to eat a "tailgate" picnic lunch before kickoff and have parties in front of television sets in each other's homes during the professional football championship game, the Super Bowl. Thousands of baseball fans flee the snow and ice of the North for a week or two each winter by making a pilgrimage to training camps in the South and Southwest to watch up close their favorite players prepare for the spring opening of the professional baseball season.

Individual competitions accompanied the growth of team sports. Shooting and fishing contests were part of the colonial experience, as were running, boxing, and horse racing. Golf and tennis emerged in the eighteen hundreds. Recent decades have given birth to a wide variety of challenging activities and contests such as sailboarding, mountain biking, and sport climbing, collectively referred to as "extreme sports."

The most popular sport in the United States is American football (which is known as football), which enjoys a huge audience and massive media coverage. Football is played at almost every level, from young children to a professional league known as the National Football League. Baseball is the second most popular sport, followed by basketball. All of these sports are televised widely on weekends and evenings and enjoy a huge following of spectators who may arrange social gatherings around the sports competitions.

Fitness

Most people in the United States work in reasonably sedentary conditions and rely on exercise either before or after work to maintain their fitness. They will either go to a gym to exercise or walk or run in their neighborhood, parks, or running trails. There are many local and national gym chains that are quite affordable.

On weekends, Americans engage in sports and other family-based activities, such as hiking, walking, swimming, boating, skiing, running, and going to parks that may include physical activity.

Physical activities and general fitness levels will also vary depending on the geographic location and the weather. According to the US Centers for Disease Control, Americans living in the South are more likely to be less active than Americans living in the West, Northeast, and Midwest regions of the country.

w. *Nutrition*

Food selection is plentiful in the United States, and therefore access to nutritious and safe foods is rarely an issue. This has created a problem whereby the average American diet exceeds the recommended intake levels of calories, sugars, refined grains, sodium, and saturated fat. You will have to take care to understand what you are eating, as many foods may be different than what you are used to.

Foods (sold in grocery stores) in the United States are required to be clearly labeled as to their nutritional content and makeup. The US Food and Drug Administration has an excellent overview of how to read a food label, and you can access it here:

www.fda.gov/food/ingredientspackaginglabeling/labelingnutrition/ucm274593.htm

x. *Domestic travel*

The United States has great highways, and you can drive almost anywhere safely. The "road trip" is a very common family activity in the United States. Driving from one part of the country to another and experiencing the changes of geography and differences between the cities and cultures is a rewarding experience.

The Northeast has better train service, and it is possible to take trains from city to city. Because of the large size of the United States, many people choose to fly from one location to another. Flights are generally reasonably priced, with a wide variety of scheduling.

y. *Marriage*

Marriage license requirements in the United States, and to receive a marriage license for your wedding ceremony, are handled at the state level.

Each state's laws differ regarding premarital procedures, including blood tests, waiting periods before marriage, and other similar requirements. Because state laws in this area have been changing rapidly—many states have recently eliminated blood tests or physical exams—you should check with your county marriage license bureau office or county clerk's office before making any wedding or travel plans.

The marriage license laws for a man and a woman to marry vary from state to state. Although there are differences between the requirements in the various states, a marriage between a man and a woman performed in one state must be recognized by every other state under the Full Faith and Credit clause of the US Constitution.Some requirements set by state law can include the following:

- A marriage license must be issued by the county clerk or clerk of the court (along with payment of a fee).
- Both the man and woman must be eighteen or older, or they must have the consent of a parent or a judge if younger.
- Proof of immunity or vaccination for certain diseases must be provided.
- Many states have done away with mandatory premarital physical exams or blood tests. Some states still require them for venereal diseases, and a few also test for rubella (also known as German measles, a disease that is very dangerous to fetuses), tuberculosis, and sickle-cell anemia.
- Proof of the termination of any prior marriages by death, judgment of dissolution (divorce), or annulment must be provided.
- Where there is a valid marriage, termination of marital status is obtained through a dissolution or divorce petition, which results in a judgment that returns both the man and the woman to the status of an unmarried (single) person.

- Sufficient mental capacity must be apparent or proved (often this is determined as the ability to enter into a contract).
- Marriage requires two consenting people. If either person cannot or does not understand what it means to be married (due to mental illness, drugs, alcohol, or other factors affecting judgment), then that person does not have the capacity to consent, and the marriage is not valid.
- The couple cannot be close blood relatives.
- Close blood relatives cannot marry, although in some states, first cousins can marry. Of the states that allow first cousins to marry, a few also require that one of the cousins no longer be able to conceive children.
- Blood tests may be required for venereal disease.
- Due to the rise in HIV and AIDS, many states now require that parties applying for a marital license must be offered an HIV test or must be provided with information on AIDS and tests available. Presently, no states require a mandatory premarital HIV/AIDS test.
- A waiting period must be satisfied from the time the marriage license is issued to the time the marriage ceremony is performed.
- Performance of a marriage ceremony must include witnesses and a person recognized by the state to have the authority to perform a ceremony (such as a priest, a rabbi, or a judge).

A religious ceremony should be conducted under the customs of the religion or, in the case of a Native American group, under the customs of the tribe. Religious ceremonies normally are conducted by religious officials such as ministers, priests, rabbis, or imams. Native American ceremonies may be presided over by a tribal chief or other designated official.

Civil ceremonies are usually conducted by judges. In some states, county clerks or other government officials may conduct civil ceremonies. Contrary to some popular legends, no state authorizes ship captains to perform marriages.

Most states require one or two witnesses to sign the marriage certificate.

Recording of the marriage license occurs after the marriage ceremony is performed.

The person who performs the marriage ceremony has a duty to send a copy of the marriage certificate to the county or state agency that records marriage certificates. Failure to send the marriage certificate to the appropriate agency does not necessarily nullify the marriage, but it may make proof of the marriage more difficult.

A marriage performed in another jurisdiction—even overseas—is usually valid in any state as long as the marriage was legal in the jurisdiction where it occurred.

Please Note: State and county marriage license requirements often change. The above information is for guidance only and should not be regarded as legal advice.

z. *Divorce*

Divorce and separation: an overview

A divorce formally dissolves a legal marriage. While married couples do not possess a constitutional or legal right to divorce, states permit divorces because to do so best serves public policy. To ensure that a particular divorce serves public policy interests, some states require a cooling off period, which prescribes a time period after legal separation through which spouses must pass before they can initiate divorce proceedings.

Courts in the United States currently recognize two types of divorces: absolute divorce, known as "divorce a vincula matrimonii," and limited divorce, known as "divorce a menso et thoro." To obtain an absolute divorce, some states require some type of evidentiary showing of misconduct or wrongdoing on one spouse's part but the trend has been for states to move to "no-fault" divorce (below). An absolute divorce is a judicial termination of a legal marriage. An absolute divorce results in the changing of both parties' statuses back to single. Limited divorces are typically referred to as separation decrees. Limited divorces result in termination of the right to cohabitate, but the court refrains from officially dissolving the marriage, and the parties' statuses remain unchanged. Some states permit conversion divorce. Conversion divorce transforms a legal separation into a legal divorce after both parties have been separated for a statutorily prescribed period of time.

Many states have enacted no-fault divorce statutes. No-fault divorce statutes do not require showing spousal misconduct and are a response to outdated divorce statutes that require proof of adultery or some other unsavory act in a court of law by the divorcing party. Nevertheless, even today, not all states have enacted no-fault divorce statutes. Instead, the court must only find that

- the relationship is no longer viable,
- irreconcilable differences have caused an irremediable breakdown of the marriage,

- discord or conflict of personalities have destroyed the legitimate goals of the marital relationship and prevents any reasonable possibility of reconciliation, or
- the marriage is irretrievably broken.

Look to various state laws to determine the divorce law within a particular jurisdiction. The Uniform Marriage and Divorce Act may provide further guidance.

Property division

Following a divorce, the court must divide the property between the spouses. Before legislatures equalized property allocation between both spouses, many divorce statutes substantially favored property allocation to the wage-earning spouse. These statutes disproportionately disadvantaged women, because during the eighteenth, nineteenth, and early twentieth centuries, the participation of women in the workplace was much less than it has become during the latter half of the twentieth century and early part of the twenty-first century. The statutes also failed to account for the contributions of the spouse as homemaker and child raiser.

Modern courts recognize two different types of property during property division proceedings: marital property and separate property. Marital property constitutes any property that the spouses acquire individually or jointly during the course of marriage. Separate property constitutes any property that one spouse purchased and possessed prior to the marriage and that did not substantially change in value during the course of the marriage because of the efforts of one or both spouses. If the separate property-owning spouse trades the property for other property or sells the property, the newly acquired property or funds in consideration of the sale remain separate property.

Alimony

Alimony refers to payments from one spouse to the other. A court can order one spouse to pay three different types of alimony: permanent alimony, temporary alimony, and rehabilitative alimony. Permanent alimony requires the payer to continue paying either for the rest of the payer's life or until the spouse receiving payments remarries. Temporary alimony requires payments over a short interval of time so that the payment recipient can stand alone once again. The period of time may only cover a period of the property division litigation. Similar to temporary alimony, rehabilitative alimony requires the payer to give the recipient short-term alimony after the property division proceedings have concluded. Rehabilitative alimony endeavors to help a spouse with lesser employability or earning capacity become adjusted to a new postmarital life.

Courts allocate alimony with the intention of permitting a spouse to maintain the standard of living to which the spouse has become accustomed. Factors affecting whether the court awards alimony include the marriage's length, the length of separation before divorce, the parties' ages, the parties' respective incomes, the parties' future financial prospects, the health of the parties, and the parties' respective faults in causing the marriage's demise.

If a couple had children together while married, a court may require one spouse to pay child support to the spouse with custody, but one should note that alimony and child support are calculated differently.

aa. *Child care*

If you work, and your children are too young to go to school, you may need to find someone to watch them while you are at work. Sometimes children in school need someone to watch them when school is over if their parents cannot be at home. If you or other family members are not able to watch your children, you need to find someone to take care of them. Do not leave young children at home alone.

Finding child care

Choosing someone to care for your children is an important decision. As you make this decision, think about the quality and cost of care. Try to find a caregiver who is close to your home or job.

There are many resources you can use to find a good child-care provider. Ask other parents, friends, and coworkers about who cares for their children. Some states have a child-care referral agency that can give you a list of state-licensed child-care programs. Licensed child-care programs meet specific requirements set by the state for the protection of your children. You also can call your local school district office to find places where other children in your neighborhood are cared for.

TIP: If you need help finding good child care in your area, the US Department of Health and Human Services has a National Child Care Information Center. Call (800) 616-2242 for information. You can also find information and answers to questions about how to choose a good program for your child at www. childcareaware.org.

Types of child care

You have a number of choices when choosing a child-care provider.

In-home care—A caregiver comes into your home to watch your children. This type of service can be expensive, because your child gets more individual attention. The quality of care depends on the person you hire.

Family child care—Your child is cared for in somebody else's home with a small group of other children. This can be less expensive than other types of child care. The quality of care depends on the people who watch your child and the number of children they are caring for in their home.

Day-care centers—Day-care centers are programs located in schools, churches or other faith-based organizations, and other places. Centers usually have several caregivers who watch larger groups of children. Centers must meet state standards, and their staff usually has special training and experience.

Head Start programs—The federal government provides funding for "Early Head Start" and "Head Start" programs for low-income families. These programs provide care and educational services to young children to get them ready for school. To learn more about these programs, call the US Department of Health and Human Services at (866) 763-6481 or visit the website www.acf.hhs.gov/programs/hsb/.

Some child-care providers will take care of children for a full day or only part of the day, depending on the parents' needs. Cost is also a factor in choosing a caregiver. Check to see if you are eligible for federal or state child-care assistance. Many states offer financial assistance to low-income parents who are working or participating in job training or education programs.

TIP: Make sure the child-care provider or program you are using is licensed or accredited. Licensed means that the program meets minimum safety and care standards set by the state. Accredited programs meet higher standards than those required for a state license.

bb. Animals and Pets

Many people in the United States have pets and raise animals both for enjoyment and as part of their business (ranching or farming). Pet ownership (based on the Humane Society of the United States statistics—www.humanesociety.org/issues/pet_overpopulation/facts/pet_ownership_statistics.html) includes 67 million households, and 164 million owned pets. This means that over 62 percent of US households have pets. By far, the most popular pets in the United States are dogs and cats. Further Humane Society statistics related to dog and cat ownership are as follows:

Dogs: 83.3 million—number of owned dogs
47 percent—the number of households that own at least one dog

Cats: 95.6 million—number of owned cats
46 percent—the number of households that own at least one cat

Bringing your pets from overseas. All such imports are subject to health, quarantine, agriculture, or wildlife requirements and prohibitions. Pets taken out of the United States and returned are subject to the same requirements as those entering for the first time. You may also contact Animal Plant Health Inspection Service (APHIS) or Veterinary Services National Center for Import and Export (NCIS) for more information by calling (301) 734-3277/8364 or at www.aphis. usda.gov/wps/portal/aphis/ourfocus/animalwelfare.

The Centers for Disease Control and Prevention (CDC) and the US Public Health Service require that pet dogs and cats brought into this country be examined at the first port of entry for evidence of diseases that can be transmitted to humans. A valid rabies (also known as *rage*) vaccination certificate must accompany dogs coming from areas not free of rabies. There is no requirement for a rabies vaccination certificate for domestic cats. Dogs from countries with screwworm must have additional paper work (you can access this list by clicking here). Service dogs do not require any additional paper work, although it is recommended to contact the Transportation Security Administration (TSA) (www.tsa.gov) and the airline you are traveling with (if traveling by air) for their requirements.

For more information visit the US Fish and Wildlife Service website: (www.fws. gov).

cc. Lawsuits and Conflicts

The framers of the US Constitution wanted the federal government to have only limited power. Therefore, they limited the kinds of cases federal courts can decide. State governments pass most laws that affect us, and thus state courts handle most disputes that govern our daily lives.

Federal courts also serve an important role. They defend many of our most basic rights, such as freedom of speech and equal protection under the law.

This is the fundamental idea behind federalism, which means a government in which power is divided between one national government and other, smaller state or regional governments.

Dual court system

There is a division of court systems in the United States: federal and state. Federal courts have limited jurisdiction over state courts. Jurisdiction means the authority of a court to hear and decide cases within an area of the law or a geographical territory.

Jurisdiction of the courts: state vs. federal

State courts are courts of general jurisdiction. They hear all the cases not specifically selected for federal courts. Just as the federal courts interpret federal laws, state courts interpret state laws. Each state gets to make and interpret its own laws. This helps the states retain power and makes sure that the national government does not become too strong.

Types of cases and federal courts

During the drafting of the Constitution, some feared that the federal courts might threaten the independence of the states and the people. To combat this fear, the framers set up a federal court system that can only hear cases in special circumstances. This is called having limited jurisdiction. Since the federal courts can only hear certain kinds of cases, most of the day-to-day cases that courts deal with happen in state courts.

The federal court system has three main levels: district courts (the trial court), circuit courts, which are the first level of appeal, and the Supreme Court of the United States, the final level of appeal in the federal system. There are ninety-four district courts, thirteen circuit courts throughout the country, and one Supreme Court.

Courts in the federal system work differently in many ways than state courts. Sometimes, the jurisdiction of state courts will overlap with that of federal courts, meaning that some cases can be brought in both courts. The plaintiff has the initial choice of bringing the case in state or federal court. However, if the plaintiff chooses state court, the defendant may sometimes choose to "remove" to federal court.

Federal judges (and Supreme Court justices) are selected by the president and confirmed "with the advice and consent" of the Senate and "shall hold their Offices during good Behavior." Judges may hold their position for the rest of their lives, but many resign or retire earlier. They may also be removed by impeachment by the House of Representatives and conviction by the Senate.

District courts

The district courts are the general trial courts of the federal court system. Each district court has at least one US district judge, appointed by the president and confirmed by the Senate for a life term. District courts handle trials within the federal court system—both civil and criminal. The districts are the same as those for the US attorneys, and the US attorney is the primary prosecutor for the federal government in his or her respective area.

Federal trial courts have also been established for a few subject-specific areas. Each federal district also has a bankruptcy court for those proceedings. Additionally, some courts have nationwide jurisdiction for issues such as tax (United States Tax Court), claims against the federal government (United States Court of Federal Claims), and international trade (United States Court of International Trade).

Circuit courts

Once the federal district court has decided a case, the case can be appealed to a United States court of appeal. There are twelve federal circuits that divide the country into different regions. The Fifth Circuit, for example, includes the states of Texas, Louisiana, and Mississippi. Cases from the district courts of those states are appealed to the United States Court of Appeals for the Fifth Circuit, which is headquartered in New Orleans, Louisiana. Additionally, the Federal Circuit Court of Appeals has a nationwide jurisdiction over very specific issues such as patents.

Each circuit court has multiple judges, ranging from six in the First Circuit to twenty-nine in the Ninth Circuit. Circuit court judges are appointed for life by the president and confirmed by the Senate. Any case may be appealed to the circuit court once the district court has finalized a decision (some issues can be appealed before a final decision by making an "interlocutory appeal"). Appeals to circuit courts are first heard by a panel consisting of three circuit court judges. Parties file briefs to the court, arguing why the trial court's decision should be affirmed or reversed. After the briefs are filed, the court will schedule oral argument, in which the lawyers come before the court to make their arguments and answer the judges' questions.

Beyond the federal circuit, a few courts have been established to deal with appeals on specific subjects such as veterans claims (United States Court of Appeals for Veterans Claims) and military matters (United States Court of Appeals for the Armed Forces).

Supreme Court of the United States

The Supreme Court of the United States is the highest court in the American judicial system, and it has the power to decide appeals on all cases brought in federal court or those brought in state court but dealing with federal law. For example, if a First Amendment freedom of speech case was decided by the highest court of a state (usually the state supreme court), the case could be appealed to the federal Supreme Court. However, if that same case were decided entirely on a state law similar to the First Amendment, the Supreme Court of the United States would not be able to consider the case.

The members of the Supreme Court are referred to as justices and, like other federal judges, they are appointed by the president and confirmed by the Senate for a life term. There are nine justices on the court—eight associate justices and one chief justice. The Constitution sets no requirements for Supreme Court justices, though all current members of the court are lawyers, and most have served as circuit court judges. Justices are also often former law professors. The chief justice acts as the administrator of the court and is chosen by the president and approved by the Congress when the position is vacant.

The Supreme Court meets in Washington, DC. The court conducts its annual term from the first Monday of October until each summer, usually ending in late June.

dd. Privacy

Privacy in the United States is a complex issue that relates to basic rights granted to all of its citizens by the Constitution, state laws and regulations, and federal laws related to privacy in the context of US government actions.

Privacy in general. The **privacy laws of the United States** embody several different legal concepts. One is the *invasion of privacy*, a tort based in common law allowing an aggrieved party to bring a lawsuit against an individual who unlawfully intrudes into his or her private affairs, discloses his or her private information, publicizes him or her in a false light, or appropriates his or her name for personal gain. Public figures have less privacy, and this is an evolving area of law as it relates to the media.

The essence of the law derives from a *right to privacy*, defined broadly as "the right to be let alone." It usually excludes personal matters or activities that may reasonably be of public interest, like those of celebrities or participants in newsworthy events. Invasion of the right to privacy can be the basis for a lawsuit for damages against the person or entity violating the right, as in the high-profile privacy lawsuit filed against the federal government by Jill Kelley, a notable privacy advocate. These include the Fourth Amendment right to be free of unwarranted search or seizure, the First Amendment right to free assembly, and the Fourteenth Amendment due process right, recognized by the Supreme Court as protecting a general right to privacy within family, marriage, motherhood, procreation, and child rearing."

The forgoing section is developed from Wikipedia (you can view the current article at: en.wikipedia.org/wiki/Privacy_laws_of_the_United_States).

Tort: a wrongful act or an infringement of a right (other than under contract) leading to civil legal liability.

Privacy laws and the US government
Freedom of Information Act

The Freedom of Information Act (FOIA) is a law that gives you the right to access information from the federal government. It is often described as the law that keeps citizens in the know about their government. Under the FOIA, agencies must disclose any information that is requested—unless that information is protected from public disclosure. The FOIA also requires that agencies automatically disclose certain information, including frequently requested records. As Congress, the president, and the Supreme Court have all recognized, the FOIA is a vital part of our democracy.

Any person can make a FOIA request for any federal agency record. To make a request, write a letter to the agency that describes the information you want, and the format you want it in, in as much detail as possible.

When you complete your letter, send it to the agency's FOIA contact.

Before you send a FOIA request, it's a good idea to look at an agency's website first to see what's already available. FOIA requires that federal agencies release certain information automatically, without the need for you to make a request.

You can request information under the privacy act by writing a letter to the agency that you believe may have a file pertaining to you. If the records you seek are about yourself, you can request them under both the FOIA and the Privacy Act of 1974.

Privacy Act of 1974

The Privacy Act of 1974 establishes certain controls over what personal information is collected by the federal government and how it is used. The Privacy Act of 1974, 5 USC § 552a (2006), which has been in effect since September 27, 1975, can generally be characterized as an omnibus "code of fair information practices" that attempts to regulate the collection, maintenance, use, and dissemination of personal information by federal executive branch agencies. However, the act's imprecise language, limited legislative history, and somewhat outdated regulatory guidelines have rendered it a difficult statute to decipher and apply. Moreover, even after more than thirty-five years of administrative and judicial analysis, numerous Privacy Act issues remain unresolved or unexplored. Adding to these interpretational difficulties is the fact that many earlier Privacy Act cases are unpublished district court decisions. A particular effort is made in this overview to clarify the existing state of the Privacy Act law while at the same time highlighting those controversial, unsettled areas where further litigation and case law development can be expected.

Privacy laws that affect business

For many companies, collecting sensitive consumer and employee information is an essential part of doing business. It's your legal responsibility to take steps to properly secure or dispose of it. Financial data, personal information about kids, and material derived from credit reports may raise additional compliance considerations. In addition, you may have legal responsibilities to victims of identity theft.

Credit reporting

Does your business use consumer reports or credit reports to evaluate customers' creditworthiness? Do you consult reports when evaluating applications for jobs, leases, or insurance? Information follows about your responsibilities under the Fair Credit Reporting Act and other laws when using, reporting, and disposing of information in those reports.

Data security

Many companies keep sensitive personal information about customers or employees in their files or on their network. Having a sound security plan in place to collect only what you need, to keep it safe, and to dispose of it securely can help you meet your legal obligations to protect that sensitive data.

ee. Innovation

The United States is one of the preeminent locations for innovation and investment in new technologies, business, and real estate.

The US economy was the world leader in the twentieth century and continues to be as it moves into the twenty-first century. The US economy remains the largest in the world, possessing a highly skilled work force, world-class companies, and according to some, the world's best higher-education system.

During the twentieth century, the pace of innovation was staggering, leading to new industries and companies, such as those in the biotech and information technology fields. Innovation also spurred growth in traditional industries, as businesses fundamentally changed the way they produced and distributed their goods and services.

In the process, the United States became the world's most innovative, most educated, and most competitive nation. Since 1980, the United States has made up 20–25 percent of the world's economy while having only about 5 percent of the world's population. The exceptional performance of the United States has helped improve the lives of its citizens, particularly during the decades after World War II. Between 1950 and 2000, incomes soared, with real disposable personal income per capita increasing 213 percent, from $9,240 to $28,899. The US economy created millions of new jobs, many in new firms and industries.

These economic gains were coupled with gains in other areas. The United States provided electricity and phone service throughout the country, built the interstate highway system, provided clean water to hundreds of millions, put men on the moon, developed the Internet, and decoded the human genome. Advances in medical science helped propel significant increases in life expectancy in the United States. Life spans, as measured at birth, rose from 47.3 years in 1900 to 77.9 in 2006. Advances in agricultural science increased the productivity of our farms by 150 percent between 1948 and 2008.

The United States has a strong tradition of scientific advancement. About 40 percent of Nobel Prizes have been awarded to US citizens, and a 2011 study placed 40 percent of the world's one hundred most innovative companies in the United States.

Successful, world-class companies are located in virtually every state in the United States; thirty-nine states are home to at least one Fortune 500 company. Within states and across state boundaries, regional innovation clusters arose. Silicon Valley became the world's information technology (IT) epicenter, but other areas also contributed significantly to the IT revolution, including the regional industry clusters in Texas, Washington State, Massachusetts, Georgia, North Carolina, Virginia, and Michigan ("Automation Alley," in Southeast Michigan). Major medical advances have been made in many states, including Alabama, California, and Pennsylvania.

ff. The environment

The environment of the United States is hugely diverse and is comprised of different climates and geologies. The United States has strict environmental laws to protect its air, water, and other natural resources including the Clean Air Act and the Clean Water Act.

Air quality. According to a recent Yale University ranking (you can access the data here: epi.yale.edu/epi/issue-ranking/air-quality) the United States has generally high air quality, listed at thirty-eighth in the world (out of 178).

Air pollution comes from many different sources. Stationary sources such as factories, power plants, and smelters; smaller sources such as dry cleaners and degreasing operations; mobile sources such as cars, buses, planes, trucks, and trains; and naturally occurring sources such as windblown dust and volcanic eruptions all contribute to air pollution. Air quality can be affected in many ways by the pollution emitted from these sources. These pollution sources can also emit a wide variety of pollutants. The EPA has these pollutants classified as the six principal pollutants (or "criteria pollutants," as they are also known). These pollutants are monitored by the EPA as well as national, state, and local organizations.

You can view the current air quality in the United States via the US government's site AirNow (www.airnow.gov).

Water quality. Water in the United States from municipal sources is mostly safe to drink and maintains a high standard compared to the rest of the world. Drinking water is regulated under federal, state, and local laws and codes.

Drinking water. According to the US Environmental Protection Agency (EPA), public drinking water systems are said to consist of community and noncommunity systems.

- A community water system (CWS) supplies water to the same population year-round. It serves at least twenty-five people at their primary residences or at least fifteen residences that are primary residences (for example, municipalities, mobile-home parks, or subdivisions).
- Noncommunity water systems are composed of transient and nontransient water systems.
  - Transient noncommunity water systems (TNCWS) provide water to twenty-five or more people for at least sixty days/year, but not to the same people and not on a regular basis (for example, gas stations, and campgrounds).

o Nontransient noncommunity water systems (NTNCWS) regularly supply water to at least twenty-five of the same people at least six months per year, but not year-round (for example, schools, factories, office buildings, and hospitals that have their own water systems).

According to the EPA, approximately 286 million Americans receive their tap water from a community water system. These public water systems are monitored and regulated as per EPA guidelines and regulations.

An estimated 15 percent of Americans, or about forty-five million people, get their water from private groundwater wells that are not subject to EPA regulations. Private groundwater wells can provide safe, clean water. However, well water can also become contaminated, leading to illness. It is the responsibility of well owners to maintain and treat their well water.

Water quality of lakes and rivers. The United States has made tremendous advances in the last twenty-five years to clean up the aquatic environment by controlling pollution from industries and sewage treatment plants. Unfortunately, not enough was done to control pollution from nonpoint (NPS) sources (i.e., agriculture, forestry, grazing, septic systems, recreation boating, urban runoff, construction, physical changes to stream channels, and habitat degradation). NPS pollution occurs when water runs over land or through the ground, picks up pollutants, and deposits them in surface waters or introduces them into groundwater.

Because of this, approximately 40 percent of US lakes and rivers surveyed by the US Environmental Protection Agency are not clean enough to meet basic uses such as fishing or swimming.

gg. Entertainment

Entertainment in the United States is as diverse as the geography, weather, and cultures it is composed of. Most Americans enjoy weekends and holidays with family—shopping, watching movies, cooking, going to see sports teams play, and visiting friends or relatives. In the summer, people tend to spend a great deal of time outside. In the winter, where the weather is cold, most activities may be indoors. Sports enjoy a high level of interest in the United States, and therefore much time is spent either watching sports (for example, baseball, football, basketball) or playing them.

It is also common for cultural groups to preserve some of the traditions and pastimes from their home cultures, and this can be seen by observation of festivals and traditions throughout the United States that have their origin elsewhere.

hh. News and media

Media in the United States refers to several different types of communications media: newspapers, magazines, cinema, radio, television, and websites. Media in the United States is widespread and open, conveying both news and opinions representing a wide range of subject matter and topics.

The two cornerstones of the media's openness in the United States are the freedom of speech and the freedom of the press.

Freedom of speech

Among other cherished values, the First Amendment protects freedom of speech. The United States Supreme Court often has struggled to determine what exactly constitutes protected speech. The following are examples of speech, both direct (words) and symbolic (actions), that the court has decided are either entitled to First Amendment protections, or not.

The First Amendment states, in relevant part, that "Congress shall make no law...abridging freedom of speech."

Freedom of speech includes the rights

1. not to speak (specifically, the right not to salute the flag)
   West Virginia Board of Education v. Barnette, 319 US 624 (1943)
2. of students to wear black armbands to school to protest a war ("Students do not shed their constitutional rights at the schoolhouse gate.")
   Tinker v. Des Moines, 393 US 503 (1969)
3. to use certain offensive words and phrases to convey political messages.
   Cohen v. California, 403 US 15 (1971)
4. to contribute money (under certain circumstances) to political campaigns
   Buckley v. Valeo, 424 US 1 (1976)
5. to advertise commercial products and professional services (with some restrictions)
   Virginia Board of Pharmacy v. Virginia Consumer Council, 425 US 748 (1976) and *Bates v. State Bar of Arizona*, 433 US 350 (1977)
6. to engage in symbolic speech, (e.g., burning the flag in protest)

Texas v. Johnson, 491 U.S. 397 (1989); *United States v. Eichmann*, 496 U.S. 310 (1990)

Freedom of speech does not include the right

1. to incite actions that would harm others (e.g., "[Shouting] 'fire' in a crowded theater.")
   Schenck v. United States, 249 US 47 (1919)
2. to make or distribute obscene materials
   Roth v. United States, 354 US 476 (1957)
3. to burn draft cards as an antiwar protest
   United States v. O'Brien, 391 US 367 (1968)
4. to permit students to print articles in a school newspaper over the objections of the school administration
   Hazelwood School District v. Kuhlmeier, 484 US 260 (1988)
5. of students to make an obscene speech at a school-sponsored event
   Bethel School District #43 v. Fraser, 478 US 675 (1986)
6. of students to advocate illegal drug use at a school-sponsored event
   Morse v. Frederick, __ US __ (2007)

Freedom of the press

Before the American Revolution, English authorities often censored the press in order to ensure that articles critical of the government were not widely circulated. The founders knew that a free press was essential for the promotion of ideas, so this protection was built into the Constitution in the Bill of Rights as the First Amendment.

The Supreme Court of the United States has been highly critical of any attempt to impose a prior restraint on the press, i.e., prohibiting a paper from publishing a story. The court has even made it harder for individuals to sue newspapers for libel and slander.

Today, suits involving freedom of the press are still prevalent in the courts.

ii. National holidays

The federal government observes the following official holidays. Most federal offices are closed on these days. If a holiday falls on a Saturday, it is observed on the preceding Friday. If a holiday falls on a Sunday, it is observed on the following Monday. Many employers also give their employees a holiday on these days:

- New Year's Day—January 1
- Birthday of Martin Luther King, Jr.—third Monday of January
- Presidents' Day—third Monday of February
- Memorial Day—last Monday of May
- Independence Day—July 4
- Labor Day—first Monday of September
- Columbus Day—second Monday of October
- Veterans Day—November 11
- Thanksgiving Day—fourth Thursday of November
- Christmas Day—December 25

A culture of immigration in the United States

We have provided a series of articles written by authors who have contributed to the State Department's Bureau of International Information Programs (IIP). The IIP engages international audiences on issues of foreign policy, society and values to help create an environment receptive to US national interests. These articles are presented and referenced in their entirety.

IIP communicates with foreign opinion makers and other publics through a wide range of print and electronic outreach materials published in English, Arabic, Chinese, French, Persian, Russian, and Spanish. IIP also provides information outreach support to US embassies and consulates in more than 140 countries worldwide.

Read more: iipdigital.usembassy.gov/iipdigital-en/aboutus.html#ixzz33rxQWTNW

American Identity: Ideas, Not Ethnicity, by Michael Jay Friedman

"Since the United States was founded in the eighteenth century, Americans have defined themselves not by their racial, religious, and ethnic identity but by their common values and belief in individual freedom."

Michael Jay Friedman is a historian and writer in the Bureau of International Information Programs of the US Department of State.

"I'm in a New York state of mind."*(Billy Joel)*

In 2000, 28.2 percent of people living in the New York metropolitan area were foreign born*(US Census Bureau).*

In 1782, barely six years after the United States of America declared its nationhood, Benjamin Franklin offered certain "Information to Those Who Would Remove to America." Among the constellation of outsize historical actors Americans came to know as their "founding fathers," Franklin was in many ways the most typically American: if George Washington was unapproachably august, Thomas Jefferson bookish, and John Adams dour, it was Franklin—that practical inventor, resourceful businessman, and ever-busy civic catalyst—who best understood that his countrymen were, as the historian Walter McDougall would later call them, a nation of hustlers. In such a land, Franklin instructed the would-be immigrant:

> People do not inquire concerning a Stranger, What is he? but, What can he do? If he has any useful Art, he is welcome; and if he exercises it, and behaves well, he will be respected by all that know him.

Franklin's remark was grounded in firsthand observation: As early as 1750, German immigrants outnumbered English stock in his home colony of Pennsylvania. The newcomers were perceived as industrious and law-abiding. Skillful farmers, they improved the land and stimulated economic growth. In 1790, when Congress set the first national standard for naturalized citizenship, it required no ethnic or religious test, no literacy test, no property requirement—just two years' residence, good character, and an oath to uphold the Constitution. Because American identity is, as Franklin understood, grounded in actions and attitudes rather than racial, religious, or ethnic identity, Americans differ from many other peoples both in how they define themselves and in the kinds of lives they choose to lead. Membership in the national community, as cultural scholar Marc Pachter has written, "[D]emands only the decision to become American."

This communal American identity embraces a pluralism that spans racial, religious, and ethnic divides. It also encompasses a strong civic commitment to individual freedom and to a representative government of limited and clearly defined powers that respects that freedom.

Melting pot or salad bowl? The American self-image has always harnessed a creative tension between pluralism and assimilation. On the one hand, immigrants traditionally have been expected to immerse themselves in the American "melting pot," a metaphor popularized by the playwright Israel Zangwill's 1908 drama *The Melting Pot*, in which one character declares:

> Understand that America is God's Crucible, the great Melting-Pot where all the races of Europe are melting and reforming! A fig for

your feuds and vendettas! Germans and Frenchmen, Irishmen and Englishmen, Jews and Russians—into the Crucible with you all! God is making the American.

Nor were Zangwill's sentiments new ones. As far back as 1782, J. Hector St. John de Crèvecoeur, a French immigrant and keen observer of American life, described his new compatriots as:

...a mixture of English, Scotch, Irish, French, Dutch, Germans, and Swedes...What, then, is the American, this new man? He is neither a European nor the descendant of a European; hence that strange mixture of blood, which you will find in no other country. I could point out to you a family whose grandfather was an Englishman, whose wife was Dutch, whose son married a French woman, and whose present four sons have now four wives of different nations. He is an American...leaving behind him all his ancient prejudices and manners...

The melting pot, however, has always existed alongside a competing model, in which each successive immigrant group retains a measure of its distinctiveness and enriches the American whole. In 1918, the public intellectual Randolph Bourne called for a "transnational America." The original English colonists, Bourne argued, "did not come to be assimilated in an American melting pot...They came to get freedom to live as they wanted to...to make their fortune in a new land." Later immigrants, he continued, had not been melted down into some kind of "tasteless, colorless" homogeneous Americanism but rather added their distinct contributions to the greater whole.

The balance between the melting pot and transnational ideals varies with time and circumstance, with neither model achieving complete dominance. Unquestionably, though, Americans have internalized a self-portrait that spans a spectrum of races, creeds, and colors. Consider the popular motion pictures depicting American troops in action during the Second World War. It became a Hollywood cliché that every platoon included a farm boy from Iowa, a Brooklyn Jew, a Polish millworker from Chicago, an Appalachian woodsman, and other diverse examples of midtwentieth-century American manhood. They strain at first to overcome their differences, but by film's end, all have bonded—as Americans. Real life could be more complicated, and not least because the African American soldier would have served in a segregated unit. Regardless, these films depict an American identity that Americans believed in—or wanted to.

Individualism and tolerance. If American identity embraces all kinds of people, it also affords them a vast menu of opportunities to make and remake themselves. Americans historically have scorned efforts to trade on "accidents of birth," such as great inherited wealth or social status. Article I of the US Constitution bars the government from granting any title of nobility, and those who cultivate an air of superiority toward their fellow Americans are commonly disparaged for "putting on airs," or worse.

Americans instead respect the "self-made" man or woman, especially when he or she has overcome great obstacles to success. The late nineteenth-century American writer Horatio Alger, deemed by the *Encyclopedia Britannica* to be perhaps the most socially influential American writer of his generation, captured this ethos in his many rags-to-riches stories, in which poor shoeshine boys or other street urchins rose, by dint of their ambition, talent, and fortitude, to wealth and fame.

In the United States, individuals craft their own definitions of success. It might be financial wealth—and many are the college dropouts working in their parents' garage in hopes of creating the next Google, Microsoft, or Apple Inc. Others might prize the joys of the sporting arena, of creating fine music or art, or of raising a loving family at home. Because Americans spurn limits, their national identity is not—cannot be—bounded by the color of their skin, by their parentage, by which house of worship they attend.

Americans hold differing political beliefs, embrace (often wildly) divergent lifestyles, and insist upon broad individual freedoms, but they do so with a remarkable degree of mutual tolerance. One key is their representative form of government: no citizen agrees with every US government decision; all know they can reverse those policies by persuading their fellow citizens to vote for change at the next election.

Another key is the powerful guarantees that protect the rights of all Americans from government overreaching. No sooner was the US Constitution ratified than Americans demanded and received the Bill of Rights: ten constitutional amendments that safeguard basic rights.

There simply *is* no one picture of a "typical" American. From the powdered-wigged Founding Fathers to the multiracial golf champion Tiger Woods, Americans share a common identity grounded in the freedom—consistent always with respecting the freedom of others—to live as they choose. The results can bemuse, intrigue, and inspire. Cambodia's biggest hip-hop star, born on a Cambodian farm, lives in Southern California. (He goes by the name "praCh.") Walt Whitman, the closest Americans have produced to a national poet, would not have been surprised. "I am large," Whitman wrote of his nation. "I contain multitudes."

Read more:
> iipdigital.usembassy.gov/st/english/publication/2008/03/20080307154033eb yessedo0.5349237.html#ixzz2zdtLAefN

The first immigrants

Immigration and US History, by Hasia Diner

"Tens of millions of immigrants over four centuries have made the United States what it is today. They came to make new lives and livelihoods in the New World; their hard work benefited themselves and their new home country."

Hasia Diner is professor of history at New York University in New York City.

Millions of women and men from around the world have decided to immigrate to the United States. That fact constitutes one of the central elements in the country's overall development, involving a process fundamental to its prenational origins, its emergence as a new and independent nation, and its subsequent rise from being an Atlantic outpost to a world power, particularly in terms of its economic growth. Immigration has made the United States of America. Like many other settler societies, the United States, before it achieved independence and afterward, relied on the flow of newcomers from abroad to people its relatively open and unsettled lands. It shared this historical reality with Canada, South Africa, Australia, New Zealand, and Argentina, among other nations.

In all of these cases the imperial powers that claimed these places had access to two of the three elements essential to fulfilling their goal of extracting natural resources from the colony. They had land and capital but lacked people to do the farming, lumbering, mining, hunting, and the like. Colonial administrators tried to use native labor, with greater or lesser success, and they abetted the escalation of the African slave trade, bringing millions of migrants, against their will, to these New World outposts.

Immigration, however, played a key role not only in making America's development possible but also in shaping the basic nature of the society. Its history falls into five distinct time periods, each of which involved varying rates of migration from distinctly different places in the world. Each reflected, and also shaped, much about the basic nature of American society and economy.

Immigration throughout time
Settlers of the New World

The first, and longest, era of immigration stretched from the seventeenth century through the early nineteenth century. Immigrants came from a range of places, including the German-speaking area of the Palatinate, France (Protestant Huguenots), and the Netherlands. Other immigrants were Jews, also from the Netherlands and from Poland, but most immigrants of this era tended to hail from the British Isles, with English, Scottish, Welsh, and Ulster Irish gravitating toward different colonies (later states) and regions.

These immigrants, usually referred to as settlers, opted in the main for farming, with the promise of cheap land a major draw for relatively impoverished Northern and Western Europeans who found themselves unable to take advantage of the modernization of their home economies. One group of immigrants deserves some special attention, because their experience sheds much light on the forces impelling migration. In this era, considerable numbers of women and men came as indentured servants. They entered into contracts with employers who specified the time and conditions of labor in exchange for passage to the New World. While they endured harsh conditions during their time of service, because of their labors, they acquired ownership of small pieces of land that they could then work as independent yeoman farmers.

Mass migration

The numbers who came during this era were relatively small. That changed, however, by the 1820s. This period ushered in the first era of mass migration. From that decade through the 1880s, about fifteen million immigrants made their way to the United States, many choosing agriculture in the Midwest and Northeast, while others flocked to cities like New York, Philadelphia, Boston, and Baltimore.

Factors in both Europe and the United States shaped this transition. The end of the Napoleonic Wars in Europe liberated young men from military service back home at the same time that industrialization and agricultural consolidation in England, Scandinavia, and much of Central Europe transformed local economies and created a class of young people who could not earn a living in the new order. Demand for immigrant labor shot up with three major developments: the settlement of the American Midwest after the inauguration of the Erie Canal in 1825, the related rise of the port of New York, and the first stirrings of industrial development in the United States, particularly in textile production, centered in New England.

Immigrants tended to cluster by group in particular neighborhoods, cities, and regions. The American Midwest, as it emerged in the middle of the nineteenth century as one of the world's most fertile agricultural regions, became home to tight-knit, relatively homogeneous communities of immigrants from Sweden, Norway, Denmark, Bohemia, and various regions of what in 1871 would become Germany.

This era saw the first large-scale arrival of Catholic immigrants to the largely Protestant United States, and these primarily Irish women and men inspired the nation's first serious bout of nativism, which combined an antipathy to immigrants in general with a fear of Catholicism and an aversion to the Irish. Particularly in the decades just before the US Civil War (1861–1865), this nativism spawned a powerful political movement and even a political party, the Know Nothings, which made anti-immigration and anti-Catholicism central to its political agenda. This period also witnessed the arrival of small numbers of Chinese men to the American West. Native-born Americans reacted intensely and negatively to their arrival, leading to the passage of the only piece of US immigration legislation that specifically named a group as the focus of restrictive policy, the Chinese Exclusion Act of 1882.

A wave becomes a flood

Gradually over the course of the decades after the Civil War, as the sources of immigration shifted, so too did the technology of ocean travel. Whereas previous immigrants had made their way to the United States via sail power, innovations in steam transportation made it possible for larger ships to bring larger loads of immigrants to the United States. The immigrants of this era tended to come from Southern and Eastern Europe, regions undergoing at the end of the nineteenth and beginning of the twentieth centuries the same economic transitions that Western and Northern Europe had earlier experienced.

As among the immigrants of the earlier period, young people predominated among the newcomers. This wave of migration, which constituted the third episode in the history of US immigration, could better be referred to as a *flood* of immigrants, as nearly twenty-five million Europeans made the voyage. Italians, Greeks, Hungarians, Poles, and others speaking Slavic languages constituted the bulk of this migration. Included among them were 2.5 to 3 million Jews.

Each group evinced a distinctive migration pattern in terms of the gender balance within the migratory pool, the permanence of their migration, their literacy rates, the balance between adults and children, and the like. But they shared one overarching characteristic: they flocked to urban destinations and made up the bulk of the US industrial labor pool, making possible the emergence of such industries as steel, coal, automobile, textile, and garment production, and enabling the United States to leap into the front ranks of the world's economic giants.

Their urban destinations, their numbers, and perhaps a fairly basic human antipathy toward foreigners led to the emergence of a second wave of organized xenophobia. By the 1890s, many Americans, particularly from the ranks of the well-off, white, native-born, considered immigration to pose a serious danger to the nation's health and security. In 1893, a group of them formed the Immigration Restriction League, and it, along with other similarly inclined organizations, began to press Congress for severe curtailment of foreign immigration.

Legislating immigration

Restriction proceeded piecemeal over the course of the late nineteenth and early twentieth centuries, but immediately after the end of World War I (1914–1918) and into the early twenties, Congress did change the nation's basic policy about immigration. The National Origins Act in 1921 (and its final form in 1924) not only restricted the number of immigrants who might enter the United States but also assigned slots according to quotas based on national origins. A complicated piece of legislation, it essentially gave preference to immigrants from Northern and Western Europe, severely limited the numbers from Eastern and Southern Europe, and declared all potential immigrants from Asia to be unworthy of entry into the United States.

The legislation excluded the Western Hemisphere from the quota system, and the twenties ushered in the penultimate era in US immigration history. Immigrants could and did move quite freely from Mexico, the Caribbean (including Jamaica, Barbados, and Haiti), and other parts of Central and South America. This era, which reflected the application of the 1924 legislation, lasted until 1965. During those forty years, the United States began to admit, case by case, limited numbers of refugees. Jewish refugees from Nazi Germany before World War II, Jewish Holocaust survivors after the war, non-Jewish displaced persons fleeing Communist rule in Eastern Europe, Hungarians seeking refuge after their failed uprising in 1956, and Cubans after the 1960 revolution managed to find haven in the United States, because their plight moved the conscience of Americans, but the basic immigration law remained in place.

The Hart-Celler Act

This all changed with passage of the Hart-Celler Act in 1965, a by-product of the civil rights revolution and a jewel in the crown of President Lyndon Johnson's Great Society programs. The measure had not been intended to stimulate immigration from Asia, the Middle East, Africa, and elsewhere in the developing world. Rather, by doing away with the racially based quota system, its authors had expected that immigrants would come from the "traditional" sending societies such as Italy, Greece, and Poland, places that labored under very small quotas in the 1924 law. The law replaced the quotas with preference categories based on family relationships and job skills, giving particular preference to potential immigrants with relatives in the United States and with occupations deemed critical by the US Department of Labor. But after 1970, following an initial influx from those European countries, immigrants began to hail from places like Korea, China, India, the Philippines, and Pakistan, as well as countries in Africa. By 2000, immigration to the United States had returned to its 1900 volume, and the United States once again became a nation formed and transformed by immigrants.

Now in the early twenty-first century, American society once again finds itself locked in a debate over immigration and the role of immigrants in American society. To some, the new immigrants have seemed unwilling or unable to assimilate into American society, too committed to maintaining their transnational connections and too far removed from core American values. As in past eras, some critics of contemporary immigrants believe that the newcomers take jobs away from Americans and put undue burdens on the educational, welfare, and health-care systems. Many participants in the debate consider a large number of illegal immigrants to pose a threat to the society's basic structure.

The immigrants, however, have supporters who point out that each new immigrant wave inspired fear, suspicion, and concern by Americans—including the children and grandchildren of earlier immigrants—and that Americans claimed, wrongly, that each group of newcomers would somehow not fit in, instead remaining wedded to their old and foreign ways. So, too, advocates of immigration and most historians of immigration argue that immigrants enrich the United States, in large measure because they provide valuable services to the nation.

In every era of US history, from colonial times in the seventeenth century through the early twenty-first century, women and men from around the world have opted for the American experience. They arrived as foreigners, bearers of languages, cultures, and religions that at times seemed alien to America's essential core. Over time, as ideas about US culture changed, the immigrants and their descendants simultaneously built ethnic communities and participated in American civic life, contributing to the nation as a whole.

Read more:
    iipdigital.usembassy.gov/st/english/publication/2008/03/20080307112004eb yessedo0.1716272.html#ixzz2zdssEkph

The Immigration Culture
New Ways of Seeing and Thinking
By Scott E. Page

"An important reason for the dynamic success of the US economy is the new ways of seeing and new ways of thinking brought to the United States by waves of immigrants from around the world."

Scott E. Page is professor of complex systems, political science, and economics at the University of Michigan in Ann Arbor, Michigan, and an external faculty member at the Santa Fe Institute in Santa Fe, New Mexico, as well as author of The Difference: How the Power of Diversity Creates Better Groups, Firms, Schools, and Societies.

The immigration policies of the United States result in a diverse nation. That diversity—differences in culture, nationality, ethnicity, and religion—contributes to the robustness and productivity of the US economy. More directly, that diversity partly explains why the United States leads the world in innovation and scientific achievement.

Immigrants prove more likely to be entrepreneurs. From 1995 to 2005, more than one-fourth of all high-tech start-ups included an immigrant as part of their leadership teams. In 2005, those firms employed nearly a half million workers and generated more than $50 billion in revenue. Among them are Intel, Google, Yahoo, Sun, and eBay.

The impact of immigrants on science is similar. More than a third of American Nobel laureates in science are immigrants. These include the 2007 Nobel Prize winners in medicine, Mario Capecchi and Oliver Smithies, who both teach at public universities.

As much ability as immigrants possess, they owe part of their success to simply bringing different skills, new ways of seeing, and new ways of thinking. When immigrants arrive in the United States, they bring with them diverse histories, narratives, cultures, and religions. They also bring a determination to succeed. Those two characteristics—cognitive diversity and desire—enable immigrants to make such substantial contributions.

Data showing the benefits of cognitive diversity are unequivocal. These benefits exist in the economy: workers in larger cities with more immigrants are the most productive in the US economy, partly due to spillovers of diverse ideas. They exist in the academy: research produced by teams of researchers from diverse backgrounds has greater impact than that of solitary scholars. And they exist in the artistic and cultural worlds: achievements in these areas depend critically on the influx of new ideas brought by immigrants.

Different perspectives

Economists, sociologists, and psychologists have begun to unpack the mechanisms through which diversity operates. Why does a diverse citizenry produce more innovations, more scientific breakthroughs, and more interesting art? The short answer is that cultural and ethnic diversity translates into more ways of seeing and thinking. Social scientists refer to these as perspectives and heuristics.

The wave of the future is not the conquest of the world by a single dogmatic creed but the liberation of the diverse energies of free nations and free men.

President John F. Kennedy

Diverse perspectives enable people to reframe a difficult problem and turn it into an easy one. New products, scientific breakthroughs, and new forms of art all arise from diverse perspectives. After seeing a plowed field, inventor Philo Farnsworth realized how to transmit images through air, an insight that led to television. We can never anticipate which perspective will lead to a breakthrough, but we can encourage diverse ways of seeing so that breakthroughs naturally occur.

Diverse ways of thinking produce smaller, more routine improvements than the bigger breakthroughs that can come from diverse perspectives. The members of any society bring and acquire an enormous collection of formal problem-solving techniques and informal rules of thumb learned from experience, education, and families. These diverse ways of thinking enable a society to make consistent, small innovations, be these in the laboratory or on the assembly line floor.

Economic growth and scientific progress depend on combining breakthroughs with sustained innovation. First, someone brings a new perspective and comes up with the idea of the bicycle, the personal computer, or the business that will allow people to run auctions on the Internet. Then others spend decades refining and improving the idea by applying different ways of thinking.

Immigration provides a steady inflow of new ways of seeing and new ways of thinking—hence the great success of immigrants in business start-ups, science, and the arts.

Leveraging diversity

The economic, scientific, and cultural benefits of immigration do not arise without the proper political, social, and economic infrastructure. Diverse societies differ from homogeneous societies in three important ways. First, diversity increases complexity. Managing complexity is never easy. This is true in economies, societies, and teams. Interactions within diverse groups and communities can at times be contentious and unpredictable.

Second, communicating different ways of seeing and thinking requires patience and tolerance. Success requires accepting difference. It requires looking beyond the color of someone's skin and hearing ideas, not accents. Most of all, success demands accepting that someone else, someone different, might have a better answer.

Third, diverse groups of people differ not only in how they think and see but also in their goals and ideals. If people disagree in their fundamental preferences—for example, if they pursue distinct national goals—then problems can arise. Diverse people cannot come together to solve a problem if they do not agree on what the problem is. People must agree on their fundamental goals and values. As strong as the evidence may be that diverse ways of seeing and thinking create enormous benefits, equally strong evidence suggests that diverse core values can create large problems.

Proper environment

In light of these three characteristics, the benefits of the diversity produced through immigration cannot accrue without the proper environment. This environment must include appropriate informal societal norms—a willingness to listen and to tolerate difference—as well as formal laws, such as those that prohibit discrimination based on identity. The hoped-for result is a national culture that, while encouraging people to think differently, also achieves broad agreement on core national goals and principles.

For example, in a healthy political system, people often disagree over how to respond to challenges. To be sure, open immigration policies create cultural, ethnic, and religious diversity. But they also produce cognitive diversity. In that cognitive diversity resides the economic, scientific, and cultural value of immigrants: new ways of seeing results in breakthroughs. A Taiwanese immigrant, David Ho, was the first to realize that while no one antiviral drug could stop AIDS, a diverse cocktail of such drugs might do it. Following through on that logic resulted in new AIDS drugs and his selection as *Time* magazine's Man of the Year in 1996. He saved millions of lives.

An extension of Ho's logic explains the value of immigration. People from different cultures bring diverse ways of seeing and thinking about the challenges and opportunities that a nation confronts. No one person can meet every challenge, but the constant influx of new and diverse ways of seeing and thinking produced by open immigration ensures that collectively we can.

Read more:
iipdigital.usembassy.gov/st/english/publication/2008/03/20080307150133eb
yessedo0.9171259.html#ixzz2zdu0Aomr

jj. The states and cities

The origin of the states

The original territory of the United States, as defined by the treaties of November 30, 1782, and September 3, 1783, with Great Britain, was bounded on the north by Canada, on the south by the Spanish Colonies of East and West Florida, on the east by the Atlantic Ocean, and on the west by the Mississippi River. It included the thirteen original colonies and the areas claimed by them.

The thirteen original states organized the federal union under the name of "The United States of America" by ratifying the Articles of Confederation and, subsequently, the Constitution. The boundaries of these states were not defined in the acts of ratification, but in general the states maintained their claim to their colonial boundaries that had been established by royal decree or by agreement. Some overlapping territorial claims were not finally settled until many years later by decision of our highest court.

The other states were admitted into the union by acts of Congress, usually upon petition of the citizens residing in the territories in question. The boundaries of these states were defined in the enabling acts. However for some states, notably Missouri and Texas, the boundaries were changed by subsequent legislation.

Regional difference

The United States is a vast place with, not surprisingly, many differences between its cultures depending on geographic location. These differences can be the type of cuisine that is commonly eaten, subtle language differences, more pronounced language differences (such as accents), voting habits, attitudes toward government, and attitudes toward other social issues.

The United States is generally described as six separate regions that share geography and some cultural attributes.

New England

Maine, New Hampshire, Vermont, Massachusetts, Connecticut, and Rhode Island

New England, the smallest region, has not been blessed with large expanses of rich farmland or a mild climate. Yet it played a dominant role in American development. From the seventeenth century until well into the nineteenth, New England was the country's cultural and economic center.

New England also supported a vibrant cultural life. The critic Van Wyck Brooks called the creation of a distinctive American literature in the first half of the nineteenth century "the flowering of New England." Education is another of the region's strongest legacies. Its cluster of top-ranking universities and colleges—including Harvard, Yale, Brown, Dartmouth, Wellesley, Smith, Mount Holyoke, Williams, Amherst, and Wesleyan—is unequaled by any other region.

In the twentieth century, most of New England's traditional industries relocated to states or foreign countries where goods can be made more cheaply. In more than a few factory towns, skilled workers have been left without jobs. The gap has been partly filled by the microelectronics and computer industries.

The Middle Atlantic

New York, New Jersey, Pennsylvania, Delaware, Washington, DC, and Maryland

The region's largest states, New York and Pennsylvania, became centers of heavy industry (iron, glass, and steel).

As heavy industry spread throughout the region, rivers such as the Hudson and Delaware were transformed into vital shipping lanes. Cities on waterways—New York on the Hudson, Philadelphia on the Delaware, and Baltimore on Chesapeake Bay—grew dramatically. New York is still the nation's largest city, its financial hub, and its cultural center.

Like New England, the Middle Atlantic region has seen much of its heavy industry relocate elsewhere. Other industries, such as drug manufacturing and communications, have taken up the slack.

The South

Virginia, West Virginia, Kentucky, Tennessee, North Carolina, South Carolina, Georgia, Florida, Alabama, Mississippi, Arkansas, Louisiana, and parts of Missouri, Texas, and Oklahoma

The South is perhaps the most distinctive and colorful American region. The American Civil War (1861–65) devastated the South socially and economically. Nevertheless, it retained its unmistakable identity.

Slavery was the most contentious issue dividing North and South. As southerners, black and white, shook off the effects of slavery and racial division, a new regional pride expressed itself under the banner of the "New South." Today the South has evolved into a manufacturing region, and high-rise buildings crowd the skylines of such cities as Atlanta and Little Rock, Arkansas. Owing to its mild weather, the South has become a mecca for retirees from other US regions and from Canada.

The Midwest

Ohio, Michigan, Indiana, Wisconsin, Illinois, Minnesota, Iowa, the northern parts of Missouri, North Dakota, South Dakota, Kansas, and Nebraska

Most of the Midwest is flat. The Mississippi River has acted as a regional lifeline, moving settlers to new homes and foodstuffs to market. The river inspired two classic American books, both written by a native Missourian, Samuel Clemens, who took the pseudonym Mark Twain: *Life on the Mississippi* and *The Adventures of Huckleberry Finn*.

Midwesterners are praised as being open, friendly, and straightforward. The region's hub is Chicago, Illinois, the nation's third largest city. This major Great Lakes port is a connecting point for rail lines and air traffic to far-flung parts of the nation and the world. At its heart stands the Sears Tower, now known as the Willis Tower, at 442 meters one of the world's ten tallest buildings.

The Southwest

Western Texas, parts of Oklahoma, New Mexico, Arizona, and Nevada

The Southwest differs from the adjoining Midwest in weather (drier), population (less dense), and ethnicity (strong Spanish American and Native American components). Outside the cities, the region is a land of open spaces, much of which is desert. The magnificent Grand Canyon is located in this region, as is Monument Valley, the starkly beautiful backdrop for many western movies. Monument Valley is within the Navajo Reservation, home of the most populous American Indian tribe. To the south and east lie dozens of other Indian reservations, including those of the Hopi, Zuni, and Apache tribes.

Population growth in the hot, arid Southwest has depended on two human artifacts: the dam and the air conditioner. Dams on the Colorado and other rivers and aqueducts such as those of the Central Arizona Project have brought water to once-small towns such as Las Vegas, Nevada; Phoenix, Arizona; and Albuquerque, New Mexico; allowing them to become metropolises. Las Vegas is renowned as one of the world's centers for gambling, while Santa Fe, New Mexico, is famous as a center for the arts, especially painting, sculpture, and opera. Another system of dams and irrigation projects waters the Central Valley of California, which is noted for producing large harvests of fruits and vegetables.

The West

Colorado, Wyoming, Montana, Utah, California, Idaho, Oregon, Washington, Alaska, and Hawaii

Americans have long regarded the West as the last frontier. Yet California has a history of European settlement older than that of most Midwestern states. Spanish priests founded missions along the California coast a few years before the outbreak of the American Revolution. In the nineteenth century, California and Oregon entered the union ahead of many states to the east.

The West is a region of scenic beauty on a grand scale. All of its eleven states are partly mountainous, and the ranges are the sources of startling contrasts. To the west of the peaks, winds from the Pacific Ocean carry enough moisture to keep the land well-watered. To the east, however, the land is very dry. Parts of western Washington State, for example, receive twenty times the amount of rain that falls on the eastern side of the state's Cascade Range.

Western cities are known for their more casual attitude and tolerance. Perhaps because so many westerners have moved there from other regions to make a new start, as a rule interpersonal relations are marked by a live-and-let-live attitude. The western economy is varied. California, for example, is both an agricultural state and a high-technology manufacturing state.

The difference between state and federal laws

Federal laws and rules apply throughout the United States. These laws apply in every state and are viewed as superior to state laws. Examples of federal law subjects are immigration, bankruptcy, federal criminal laws, civil rights, and patents and copyrights.

Each state also has its own system of laws and courts that handle items that are not addressed at the federal level (in some cases these laws conflict, and in those cases they must go to federal court to decide the matter). These laws generally deal with issues such as nonfederal criminal matters, real estate and business transactions, contracts, probate, welfare and public assistance, divorce, and family matters such as child custody, personal injuries, and workers compensation.

States' rights

Under the powers of the US Constitution, the national and state governments have different exclusive powers. This was designed to limit the power of the federal government. The exclusive powers of the federal government and state governments are detailed below:

Exclusive powers of the federal government include

- printing money,
- regulating interstate (between the states) and international trade,
- making treaties and conducting foreign policy
- declaring war,
- providing for an army and navy,
- establishing post offices,
- making laws necessary and proper to carry out these powers.

Exclusive powers of the state governments include

- issuing licenses,
- regulating intrastate (within the state) businesses,
- conducting elections,
- establishing local governments,
- ratifying amendments to the Constitution,
- taking measures for public health and safety,
- possibly exerting powers the Constitution does not delegate to the federal government or prohibit the states from using.

Cities and counties

A city is a large permanent settlement of people. In the United States, it may have its own laws, courts, police department, government, water supply, trash services, and medical care services.

Counties are ways of dividing up land for political reasons and are generally larger than cities. Counties may contain several cities. Counties also may have their own law enforcement officers, fire department and other services; however, they will supply these services to the entire county as opposed to just the cities. While most states refer to counties as such some states may not. The counties in Louisiana are called parishes, in Alaska they are known as boroughs, and the District of Columbia is roughly equivalent to a county.

Local law and ordinances

Local laws and ordinances are laws that are passed by different cities, towns, municipalities, villages, counties, townships, and commonwealth territories. These laws are usually focused on local safety and zoning.

kk. Major metropolitan areas in the United States and their business environments

Population

The United States has some of the largest and most productive metropolitan areas in the world. Listed below are the top ten metropolitan areas in the United States by population (according to the 2010 US Census):

1. New York metropolitan area—23,076,664
2. Los Angeles metropolitan area—17,877,006
3. Chicago metropolitan area—9,840,929
4. Washington (DC) metropolitan area—9,051,961
5. San Jose/San Francisco/Oakland metropolitan area—8,153,696
6. Boston metropolitan area—7,893,376
7. Philadelphia metropolitan area—7,067,807
8. Dallas metropolitan area—6,817,483
9. Miami metropolitan area—6,166,766
10. Houston metropolitan area—6,114,562

Business environment

The United States Department of Commerce is a wealth of information related to the US business environment. Below are the Q&As from their website (you can access the original here: www.selectusa.commerce.gov/frequently-asked-questions):

Q: What sort of business opportunities exist in the US market?

A: The United States has the largest economy in the world, with a per capita GDP of approximately $51,371 and a population of *over 317 million people*. The systems of regulation and taxation in the United States give foreign investors ample operational freedom. The fifty states, District of Columbia, and the five US territories comprise a continental economy in which virtually every industrial sector has a major presence—regardless of your company's business function, you will find great opportunity in the vibrant, multifaceted US economy.

Q: How do opportunities for success in the United States compare to those in other countries?

A: Because of the size, dynamism, and international linkages that characterize the US economy, there is arguably much more opportunity for success in the

United States than in any other country in the world. The sheer size of the US market means that even firms with a small total market share can realize significant revenue streams and profits in the United States. Furthermore, US firms have easy access to export markets since the United States is one of the most internationally engaged economies in the world. The United States is a superior platform for companies in virtually every industry, both for sales to US consumers and as a production base for export to global markets.

Q: Tell me about intellectual property rights (IPR) protections in the United States.

A: The United States has a world-leading intellectual property rights (IPR) regime. Talented people and innovative companies are more successful in the United States than many other countries in the world, because their innovations are strongly protected, enabling them to reap greater rewards. Investors from around the world come to the United States to invest in research and development and to commercialize the results of their creativity. The United States provides a strong regime of intellectual property rights protection and enforcement. Of the 277,835 patents granted by the US Patent Office in 2012, 52 percent of the applications originated in a foreign country. Many US and foreign firms partner with America's world-class universities to develop and profit from innovations in engineering, bioscience, and physics.

Q: Where can I obtain US market research?

A: The United States provides potential investors with a variety of investment opportunities, and chances of an investment's success are greatly increased when companies carry out due diligence and market research. SelectUSA's website provides industry snapshots that give an overview of opportunities in specific US sectors.

General information on industry trends within the United States can be found at the Bureau of Economic Analysis's (BEA) Industry Economic Accounts page (www.bea.gov).

A breakdown of inward foreign direct investment by industry can also be found through the Bureau of Economic Analysis.

Examining exports and imports over time can also give a sense of industry trends. US export and import data can be found at TradeStats Express (http://tse.export.gov/TSE/TSEhome.aspx), through the International Trade Administration.

Many reputable private firms—from consulting companies to banks to market research firms—already compile industry analyses, usually available for a fee. Industry associations can also provide valuable information to members.

Q: Is skilled labor for my enterprise available in the United States?

A: Through higher education and workforce training, the United States cultivates one of the most skilled labor markets in the world. Seven of the top ten universities in the world are located in the United States, which is home to more than four thousand universities and colleges. Moreover, the US attracts students from across the globe, and more than 819,644 international students were enrolled in American institutions in the 2012–2013 academic year. There is an extensive network of community colleges that can help firms train their workforce for new job skills in an ever-changing marketplace, many of which have tailored training programs to investors who locate facilities in their area. Federal, state, and local governments also spend billions of dollars on workforce training each year. Importantly, the United States also has a large pool of skilled workers in the manufacturing sector.

Q: How does the US transportation infrastructure network compare to that of other leading nations?

A: The United States is well-connected to the world via its network of ports, airports, roads, and railways. In 2012, 46.9 percent of international trade traveled by water, nearly 25 percent by air, and the remainder by surface and additional modes. US cities, regions, and rural areas are connected by over forty-seven thousand miles of interstate highway and 140,000 miles of freight railroad, as well as tens of thousands of miles of state and local highways and roads. As of 2011, the United States had 547 certificated civil airports and was home to six of the world's top twenty busiest passenger airports and seven of the world's top twenty busiest cargo airports in 2011. US ports processed over 27 million twenty-foot equivalent units (TEUs) in 2010, with the ten largest ports handling 59.7 percent of all shipments. US transportation is highly intermodal, with hubs connecting the rich networks of road, rail, ports, and airports that crisscross the country.

II. Cost of living

National averages

The term "cost of living" describes how much you will pay for housing, food, clothing, and other everyday items. It is calculated by finding prices for these goods and services based on a sample.

According to Numbeo (an independent aggregator of cost of living, property price, crime, and health-care information and statistics) the cost of living in the United States as represented by prices are as follows (you can access the original data here: www.numbeo.com/cost-of-living/country_result.jsp?country=United+States)

Restaurants

Meal, inexpensive restaurant	$10.00
Meal for two, midrange restaurant, three-course	$45.00
Combo meal at McDonalds or similar	$6.40
Domestic beer (0.5 liter draught)	$3.50
Imported beer (0.33 liter bottle)	$5.00
Cappuccino (regular)	$3.65
Coke/Pepsi (0.33 liter bottle)	$1.59
Water (0.33 liter bottle)	$1.27

Markets

Milk (regular), (1 liter)	$1.00
Loaf of Fresh White Bread (500 g)	$2.40
Rice (white), (1 kg)	$2.92
Eggs (12)	$2.26
Local cheese (1 kg)	$9.47
Chicken breasts, boneless, skinless (1 kg)	$7.70
Apples (1 kg)	$3.72
Oranges (1 kg)	$3.63
Tomato (1 kg)	$3.75
Potato (1 kg)	$2.38
Lettuce (1 head)	$1.57
Water (1.5 liter bottle)	$1.76
Bottle of wine (midrange)	$12.00
Domestic beer (0.5 liter bottle)	$2.31
Imported beer (0.33 liter bottle)	$3.29
Pack of cigarettes (Marlboro)	$6.00
Transportation	
One-way ticket (local transport)	$2.00
Monthly pass (regular price)	$66.00
Taxi start (normal tariff)	$3.00
Taxi one km (normal tariff)	$1.55
Taxi one hour waiting (normal tariff)	$28.75
Gasoline (one liter)	$0.96

Utilities (monthly)

Basic (electricity, heating, water, garbage) for 85 m² apartment	$162.21

One min. of prepaid mobile tariff local (no discounts or plans)	$0.15
Internet (6 Mbps, unlimited data, cable/ADSL)	$46.29

Sports and leisure

Fitness club, monthly fee for one adult	$39.38
Tennis court rent (one hour on weekend)	$18.75
Cinema, international release, one seat	$10.00

Clothing and shoes

One pair of jeans (Levis 501 or similar)	$40.94
One summer dress in a chain store (Zara, H&M, etc.)	$36.49
One pair of Nike shoes	$76.67
One pair of men's leather shoes	$83.62

Rent per month

Apartment (one bedroom) in city center	$997.07
Apartment (one bedroom) outside of center	$753.36
Apartment (three bedrooms) in city center	$1,703.47
Apartment (three bedrooms) outside of center	$1,283.45

Buy apartment price

Price per square meter to buy apartment in city center	$1,877.90
Price per square meter to buy apartment outside of center	$1,226.60

Salaries and financing

Average monthly disposable salary (after tax)	$ 3,269.44
Mortgage interest rate in percentages, yearly	4.2

These data are based on 73,246 entries in the past eighteen months from 8323 different contributors.

Last update: June 2014

By state

The cost of living in the United States varies by state. This can be due to differences in taxation, logistics costs, and many other factors. According to the Missouri Department of Economic Development, the average cost of living in 2013 was as follows for the states as compared to the national average:

2013 Annual Average Cost of Living

State	Rank	Index	Grocery	Housing	Utilities	Transport	Heath	Misc
Mississippi	1	89.1	87.8	76.3	93.2	96.6	91.6	95.2
Nebraska	2	89.5	87.1	80.9	94.9	95.1	93.6	92.9
Idaho	3	89.8	83.2	78	93.8	101.3	99.3	94.7
Kentucky	4	90.1	85.8	78.8	98.5	97.1	94.1	94.8
Tennessee	5	90.2	88.2	80.2	89.4	93.4	89.7	97.8
Oklahoma	6	90.4	88.5	81.7	91.6	95.2	96	94.9
Indiana	7	90.6	86.4	81.3	91.1	99	97.3	95.1
Utah	8	91.1	89.5	83.2	84.2	97.2	92.5	97.5
Arkansas	9	91.6	89.7	83.1	95.7	92.5	87.2	98.1
Texas	10	91.8	87.4	84.3	93.7	96.4	95.4	96.8
Kansas	11	92	87.3	84.7	94.7	94	94.3	97.7
Iowa	12	92.1	87.2	88.2	91.6	97.8	95.4	94.6
New Mexico	13	92.3	89.3	87.5	88.5	100.2	97.5	94.8
Alabama	14	92.4	93.8	78.5	103.8	94	86.7	99.7
Ohio	15	92.5	91.6	82.8	96.8	100	94.1	96
Missouri	16	92.8	92.4	80.2	105.4	95.9	97.1	97.4
Georgia	17	92.9	91.7	81.9	100.3	97.4	98	97.3
Michigan	18	94.8	84.8	89.2	102.8	103.5	96.7	97.3
Louisiana	19	95	94.1	92.4	92.7	97.1	96.3	97.1
Nevada	20	95.5	93.6	94.6	79.2	102.2	98.6	98.8
South Carolina	21	95.6	100.1	82.6	105.8	95	98.9	100.7
Illinois	22	95.6	89.4	91	97.6	104.6	99.5	97.3
North Carolina	23	95.9	101.5	86.2	99.2	96.5	105.7	98.6
Virginia	24	96.2	92.5	93.4	101.8	92.9	98.3	99.2
Wisconsin	25	96.5	91.3	89.4	102.2	100.4	111	98.9
Wyoming	26	96.7	99.4	97.1	100	91.2	104	95.3
West Virginia	27	97.2	91.9	95.4	97.9	104.6	97.7	97.5
Florida	28	98.2	96.6	95.1	97.1	103.2	99	99.4
Montana	29	98.4	96.7	99.6	92.1	93.8	106.9	100.6
Colorado	30	99.5	93.5	105.8	94.5	98.9	101.9	98.4

South Dakota	31	99.6	91.4	106.8	98.2	93.7	96.8	100.3
North Dakota	32	99.9	96	102.3	83.5	101.2	111.1	102.5
Pennsylvania	33	100.7	99.1	96.6	111	102.2	95.9	101.6
Arizona	34	101.9	96.8	108.6	95.3	99.8	100.6	101.5
Minnesota	35	101.9	107.2	97.2	95.8	101.4	104.1	105.2
Washington	36	102.6	95.4	105.9	89.2	107.2	116	103.2
Oregon	37	106.8	96.8	116.4	96.7	114.9	113.4	102.2
Delaware	38	107.2	111.6	99.8	116.2	105	101.5	110.1
Maine	39	110.6	103.3	120.4	85.4	110	122.1	111.8
Maryland	40	119.9	106.2	176.8	109.2	100.6	96	94.7
Vermont	41	120.5	111.2	145.1	128.5	110.1	107.7	108.4
New Hampshire	42	120.7	98.8	138.9	122.7	101.5	117.9	122.4
Massachusetts	43	122.1	110.2	137.4	131	104.2	125	118.6
Rhode Island	44	125.7	107.2	139.8	133.1	104.5	118.5	129
California	45	128.1	106	187	108.3	113.1	109.7	104.9
New Jersey	46	130	114	170.1	129.6	109.9	105.7	116.1
Alaska	47	131.4	120.5	144.9	162.5	116.3	146.1	119.3
Connecticut	48	132.6	115.2	166.2	120.7	119.3	118.8	123.8
New York	49	136.4	108.7	204.3	113.2	111.7	104.1	115.3
District of Columbia	50	140.1	108.2	249.3	104.1	105.8	98.8	96.9
Hawaii	51	156.9	157.6	209.7	192.8	128.6	113.8	121.1
Grand Total		100	100	100	100	100	100	100

mm. Government

We the people: The role of the citizen in the United States

In the United States, the government gets its power to govern from the people. We have a government of the people, by the people, and for the people. Citizens in the United States shape their government and its policies, so they must learn about important public issues and get involved in their communities. Citizens vote in free elections to choose important government officials, such as the president, vice president, senators, and representatives. All citizens can call their elected officials to express an opinion, ask for information, or get help with specific issues.

Our government is based on several important values: freedom, opportunity, equality, and justice. Americans share these values, and these values give us a common civic identity.

Government in the United States protects the rights of each person. The United States is made up of people from different backgrounds, cultures, and religions. Our government and laws are organized so that citizens from different backgrounds and with different beliefs all have the same rights. No one can be punished or harmed for having an opinion or belief that is different from that of most other people.

How the federal government works

The Constitution created three branches for the federal government, so that power would be balanced. The three branches have separate responsibilities. We call this the system of "checks and balances." No single branch of government can become too powerful, because it is balanced by the other two branches. The three branches of the federal government are

- the legislative branch: the US Congress and related offices;
- the executive branch: the president, vice president, and departments of the federal government;
- the judicial branch: the Supreme Court of the United States and federal courts across the country.

Voting

Voter eligibility. To be eligible to vote, you must be a US citizen. In most states, you must be eighteen years old to vote, but some states do allow seventeen-year-olds to vote. States also have their own residency requirements to vote. For additional information about state-specific requirements and voter eligibility, contact your state election office (http://www.eac.gov/voter_resources/contact_your_state.aspx).

How to register or change your registration. In almost all states, you can register by mail to vote using the National Mail Voter Registration Form: http://www.eac.gov/voter_resources/register_to_vote.aspx

North Dakota, Wyoming, American Samoa, Guam, Puerto Rico, and the US Virgin Islands do not accept the National Mail Voter Registration Form. New Hampshire accepts it only as a request for an absentee voter mail-in registration form. If you live in one of these states, please check with your state election office to find out how to register to vote.

You may also use the National Mail Voter Registration Form to update your registration if you changed your name or your address, or to register with a political party.

You may be able to apply to register to vote in person at the following public facilities:

- state or local voter registration and/or election offices (http://www.eac.gov/voter_resources/contact_your_state.aspx)
- the Department of Motor Vehicles (http://www.usa.gov/Topics/Motor-Vehicles.shtml)
- public assistance agencies
- armed services recruitment centers (http://www.todaysmilitary.com/contact-a-recruiter)
- state-funded programs that serve people with disabilities
- any other public facility that a state has designated as a voter registration agency. In some states, you can also register online to vote. To learn if your state offers online voter registration, please contact your state election office.

The legislative branch: Congress

Citizens of the United States vote in free elections to choose people to represent them in the US Congress. Congress has the responsibility of making the laws for our nation. Congress is made up of the House of Representatives and the Senate.

In the United States, everyone can contact their elected representative and senators. To write to your representative:

The Honorable (add representative's full name)
US House of Representatives
Washington, DC 20515

To write to your senator:

The Honorable (add senator's full name)
United States Senate
Washington, DC 20510

You can visit the websites of Congress to learn about current activities in the House and Senate and about your own representative and senators, including their website addresses.

For the House of Representatives, visit www.house.gov

For the Senate, visit www.senate.gov

Senators and members of the House of Representatives can serve in Congress for an unlimited period of time.

The judicial branch: the Supreme Court

The Constitution created the Supreme Court, the highest court in the United States. There are nine judges on the Supreme Court. They are called justices. The president chooses the members of the Supreme Court, and they serve as long as they are able. The Supreme Court can overrule both state and federal laws if they conflict with the Constitution. There are other federal courts, such as the district courts and the circuit courts of appeals. To learn more about the Supreme Court, visit www.supremecourtus.gov.

The executive branch: the president

The president is the leader of the executive branch and is responsible for upholding and enforcing the laws of the country. The president has many other responsibilities, too, such as setting national policies, proposing laws to Congress, and choosing high-level officials and members of the Supreme Court. The president also is the leader of the US military and may be called the commander in chief. People vote in elections for the president and vice president every four years. The president can only serve in office for two four-year terms. The vice president becomes president if the president becomes disabled or dies.

Military: the secretary of defense

The secretary of defense is the principal defense policy adviser to the president. Under the direction of the president, the secretary exercises authority, direction, and control over the Department of Defense. The deputy secretary, the second-highest ranking official in the DoD, is delegated full power and authority to act for the secretary and to exercise the powers of the secretary on any and all matters for which the secretary is authorized to act.

Today, the Department of Defense is not only in charge of the military, but it also employs a civilian force of thousands. With over 1.4 million men and women on active duty and 718,000 civilian personnel, it is the nation's largest employer.

Another 1.1 million serve in the National Guard and reserve forces. More than two million military retirees and their family members receive benefits.

Headquarters of the Department of Defense: The Pentagon

The Pentagon is one of the world's largest office buildings. Built during the early years of World War II, it is still thought of as one of the most efficient office buildings in the world. Despite 17.5 miles of corridors, it takes only seven minutes to walk between any two points in the building.

It is the mission of the Department of Defense (DoD) to provide the military forces needed to deter war, protect the security of our country, and support the overall mission of the Department of Defense by providing official, timely, and accurate information about defense policies, organizations, functions, and operations. In addition, Defense.gov is the single unified starting point for finding military information online.

US Army

The army is the nation's principal land force. It provides combat operations on land in all environments and types of terrain, including complex urban environments, in order to defeat enemy ground forces, and seize, occupy, and defend land areas. It operates within more than 120 countries to date.

Personnel

- 488,000 active duty soldiers deployed worldwide
- 189,000 army reserves
- 346,000 National Guard

US Navy

The navy fights on the water, under the water, and over the water. Every day, tens of thousands of sailors and marines and about 40 percent of all navy ships are far from home.

Current responsibilities include

- protecting allies from ballistic missile attack in the Pacific, Arabian Gulf, and the Mediterranean;
- catching drug smugglers in the Caribbean;
- building new partnerships in South America, Southeast Asia, and Africa;

- flying our navy planes, launched from carriers sailing the Indian Ocean, for about one-third of the close-air support missions that protect our soldiers and marines on the ground in Afghanistan.

Personnel

- 330,000 active duty
- 120,000 reservists deployed

US Marine Corps

The US Marine Corps is responsible for providing power projection from the sea, utilizing the mobility of the US Navy to rapidly deliver combined-arms task forces to global crises. A part of the Department of the Navy, the marines are the smallest of the US armed forces corps in the Department of Defense.

Current responsibilities include serving as sea-based, integrated air-ground units for contingency and combat operations, and flying fighter jets, based on navy amphibious ships, nicknamed "big decks," as well as driving tanks and ground vehicles.

Personnel

- 190,000 active duty marines
- 40,000 US Marine Corps reservists

US Air Force

The US Air Force mission is to fly, fight, and win…in air, space, and cyberspace. The air force is the newest service, formed only in 1947 when the US Army Air Corps became an independent air force.

The US Air Force has three core competencies: developing airmen, technology-to-war fighting, and integrating operations.

Current responsibilities include protecting American airspace after September 11, and supporting air and ground combat ops since 2001 for Operation Enduring Freedom.

Personnel

- 324,000 active duty
- 177,000 Air National Guard and reservists

US Coast Guard

The Coast Guard is a military, multimission, maritime service with maritime safety and security operations, marine environmental protection, waterways management, and regulatory functions, as well as homeland security and national defense operations.

The Coast Guard provides direct support to the Department of Defense and functions as a specialized service in the Department of the Navy in a time of declared war or by executive order. Located within the Department of Homeland Security, the Coast Guard is the only military service with statutory authority to enforce domestic US laws.

Current responsibilities include port, waterways, and coastal security; drug and migrant interdiction; aids to navigation; performing search and rescue operations and marine environmental protection; and providing defense readiness and law enforcement operations.

Personnel

- 42,390 active-duty members
- 6,945 reservists

US National Guard

The US Army and Air Force National Guard, organized by state, are the first military responders for domestic crises like Hurricane Katrina. The Guard provides 35–40 percent of the army and air force operational forces, serving in locations like Afghanistan and the Horn of Africa. Members of the National Guard, as well as the reserves, return to their civilian jobs in between activation periods.

Current responsibilities include providing wartime military support, and performing humanitarian, peacekeeping, and homeland security missions.

Personnel

- 460,000 soldiers and airmen located in over thirty-three hundred American communities

Departments (DOJ, DS, DHS, Treasury)

The cabinet

The tradition of the cabinet dates back to the beginnings of the presidency itself. Established in Article II, Section 2, of the Constitution, the cabinet's role is to advise the president on any subject he may require, relating to the duties of each member's respective office.

The cabinet includes the vice president and the heads of fifteen executive departments—the secretaries of Agriculture, Commerce, Defense, Education, Energy, Health and Human Services, Homeland Security, Housing and Urban Development, Interior, Labor, State, Transportation, Treasury, and Veterans Affairs, as well as the attorney general.

The federal system

A country of many governments

The powers not delegated to the United States by the Constitution, nor prohibited by it to the states, are reserved to the states respectively, or to the people.

The US Constitution, Amendment X, 1789

The federal entity created by the Constitution is the dominant feature of the American governmental system. But the system itself is in reality a mosaic, composed of thousands of smaller units—building blocks that together make up the whole. There are fifty state governments plus the government of the District of Columbia, and farther down the ladder are still smaller units that govern counties, cities, towns, and villages.

This multiplicity of governmental units is best understood in terms of the evolution of the United States. The federal system, it has been seen, was the last step in an evolutionary process. Prior to the Constitution, there were the governments of the separate colonies (later states) and, prior to those, the governments of counties and smaller units. One of the first tasks accomplished by the early English settlers was the creation of governmental units for the tiny settlements they established along the Atlantic coast. Even before the Pilgrims disembarked from their ship in 1620, they formulated the Mayflower Compact, the first written American constitution. And as the new nation pushed westward, each frontier outpost created its own government to manage its affairs.

The drafters of the US Constitution left this multilayered governmental system untouched. While they made the national structure supreme, they wisely recognized the need for a series of governments more directly in contact with the people and more keenly attuned to their needs. Thus, certain functions—such as defense, currency regulation, and foreign relations—could only be managed by a strong centralized government. But others—such as sanitation, education, and local transportation—could be better served by local jurisdictions.

State government

Before their independence, colonies were governed separately by the British Crown. In the early years of the republic, prior to the adoption of the Constitution, each state was virtually an autonomous unit. The delegates to the Constitutional Convention sought a stronger, more viable federal union, but they were also intent on safeguarding the rights of the states.

In general, matters that lie entirely within state borders are the exclusive concern of state governments. These include internal communications; regulations relating to property, industry, business, and public utilities; the state criminal code; and working conditions within the state. Within this context, the federal government requires that state governments must be democratic in form and that they adopt no laws that contradict or violate the federal Constitution or the laws and treaties of the United States.

There are, of course, many areas of overlap between state and federal jurisdictions. Particularly in recent years, the federal government has assumed ever-broadening responsibility in such matters as health, education, welfare, transportation, and housing and urban development. But where the federal government exercises such responsibility in the states, programs are usually adopted on the basis of cooperation between the two levels of government, rather than as an imposition from above.

Like the national government, state governments have three branches: executive, legislative, and judicial; these are roughly equivalent in function and scope to their national counterparts. The chief executive of a state is the governor, elected by popular vote, typically for a four-year term (although in a few states, the term is two years). Except for Nebraska, which has a single legislative body, all states have a bicameral legislature, with the upper house usually called the senate and the lower house called the house of representatives, the house of delegates, or the general assembly. In most states, senators serve four-year terms, and members of the lower house serve two-year terms.

The constitutions of the various states differ in some details but generally follow a pattern similar to that of the federal Constitution, including a statement of the rights of the people and a plan for organizing the government. On such matters as the operation of businesses, banks, public utilities, and charitable institutions, state constitutions are often more detailed and explicit than the federal one. Each state constitution, however, provides that the final authority belongs to the people and sets certain standards and principles as the foundation of government.

County government

The county is a subdivision of the state, usually—but not always—containing two or more townships and several villages. New York City is so large that it is divided into five boroughs, each a county in its own right: the Bronx, Manhattan, Brooklyn, Queens, and Staten Island. On the other hand, Los Angeles County, with nearly ten million people, includes eighty-eight municipalities with their own local governments as well as large unincorporated areas that the county governs directly.

In most US counties, one town or city is designated as the county seat, and this is where the government offices are located and where the board of commissioners or supervisors meets. In small counties, boards are chosen by the county as a whole; in the larger ones, supervisors represent separate districts or townships. The board levies taxes; borrows and appropriates money; fixes the salaries of county employees; supervises elections; builds and maintains highways and bridges; and administers national, state, and county welfare programs.

Town and village government

Thousands of municipal jurisdictions too small to qualify as city governments are chartered as towns and villages. They deal with local needs, such as paving and lighting the streets; ensuring a water supply; providing police and fire protection; establishing local health regulations; arranging for garbage, sewage, and other waste disposal; collecting local taxes to support governmental operations; and directly administering the local school system.

The government is usually entrusted to an elected board or council, which may be known by a variety of names: town or village council, board of selectmen, board of supervisors, board of commissioners. The board may have a chairperson or president who functions as chief executive officer, or there may be an elected mayor. Governmental employees may include a clerk, treasurer, police and fire officers, and health and welfare officers.

One unique aspect of local government, found mostly in the New England region of the United States, is the town meeting. Once a year—sometimes more often if needed—the registered voters of the town meet in open session to elect officers, debate local issues, and pass laws for operating the government. As a body, they decide on road construction and repair, construction of public buildings and facilities, tax rates, and the town budget. The town meeting, which has existed for more than two centuries, is often cited as the purest form of direct democracy, in which the governmental power is not delegated, but is exercised directly and regularly by all the people.

City and local government

Once predominantly rural, the United States is today a highly urbanized country, with 81 percent of its citizens now living in towns, large cities, or suburbs of cities. This statistic makes city governments critically important in the overall pattern of American government. To a greater extent than on the federal or state level, the city directly serves the needs of the people, providing everything from police and fire protection to sanitary codes, health regulations, education, public transportation, and housing.

The business of running major US cities is enormously complex. In terms of population alone, New York City is larger than thirty-nine of the fifty states. It is often said that, next to the presidency, the most difficult executive position in the country is that of mayor of New York.

City governments are chartered by states, and their charters detail the objectives and powers of the municipal government. But in many respects, the cities function independently of the states. For most big cities, however, cooperation with both state and federal organizations is essential to meeting the needs of their residents.

Types of city governments vary widely across the nation. However, almost all have some kind of central council, elected by the voters, and an executive officer, assisted by various department heads, to manage the city's affairs.

Americans have come to rely on their governments to perform a wide variety of tasks that, in the early days of the republic, people did for themselves. In colonial days, there were few police officers or fire fighters, even in the large cities; governments provided neither streetlights nor street cleaners. To a large extent, people protected their own property and saw to their families' needs.

Now, meeting these needs is seen as the responsibility of the whole community, acting through government. Even in small towns, the police, fire, welfare, and health department functions are exercised by governments. Hence, the bewildering array of jurisdictions.

Read more:
  iipdigital.usembassy.gov/st/english/publication/2008/06/20080624223940ea ifas0.2905542.html#ixzz2zdnhPjeZ

nn. Common misperceptions

Economic realities of the average family

By international standards, the average US family is quite prosperous, earning an average of $50,054 (according to the US Census Bureau) in 2011. While this amount may seem significant, in some locations this may be barely enough money to support a family of four (especially in a location with very high real-estate costs) and save anything for retirement. Therefore, it is important when choosing a place to live that you take as many things into consideration as possible, including taxes and the cost of living.

There are some excellent online resources on analyzing the cost of living in different cities, such as

- www.money.cnn.com/calculator/pf/cost-of-living/
- www.payscale.com/cost-of-living-calculator
- www.bankrate.com/calculators/savings/moving-cost-of-living-calculator. aspx

Work ethic

The concept of the American work ethic is different in different regions in the United States. In general, most Americans consider themselves hardworking; however, on an international scale, American workers are probably somewhere in the middle. Americans believe that their career should be not only productive but also satisfying.

The American lunch break is usually only thirty minutes (one hour when legally mandated), and many workers now eat their lunch at their desks.

Chapter 4:

EDUCATION

To make sure all children are prepared to succeed, the United States provides free public education. This section tells you how to sign your children up for school. You will learn how US schools work and how to help your children learn.

a. Enrolling your child in school

Most public schools in the United States are coeducational. Coeducational means that girls and boys attend classes together. The United States has compulsory school attendance laws. This means that state laws require all children ages five to sixteen to attend school in most states. Check with your state department of education to find out the required ages for school attendance in your state.

You can send your child to a public or private school. In most states, parents may also teach their children at home. This is called "homeschooling." Public schools are free and do not offer religious instruction. What your children learn in public school is set by the state. However, local teachers and parents decide how it is taught. Your federal and state income taxes and your local property taxes pay for these schools.

Students must pay a fee (called "tuition") to attend private schools. Religious groups run many private schools. Some are coeducational. Some are only for boys or only for girls. Some offer financial help for students who cannot pay the tuition.

Most American children are in school for twelve years. Your children will be placed in a class (called a "grade") based on their ages and how much previous education they have. Sometimes a school may give your child a test to decide what grade he or she should be in.

b. Preschool

Preschool refers to the stage of schooling that is considered early education, generally for children between the ages of three and five. These may be privately run or government run and are generally prior to when the formal schooling system begins.

Preschools generally operate for shorter hours than a traditional day care facility and are usually more focused on academic learning to help the child transition smoothly into kindergarten. Most preschools are not mandated by law and are not considered part of the primary education.

c. Primary school

Primary school refers to the first eight years of formal education for children in the United States. This begins at kindergarten (most children are around age five at the time they begin kindergarten) and continues until the children complete grade six.

Most students' classes are arranged around a homeroom, with one or two teachers.

Most children finish with their primary education around age eleven. Once the child completes primary school they advance to middle school.

d. Middle school and high school

Middle school usually consists of seventh, eighth, and sometimes ninth grade.

High school usually runs from eighth or ninth to twelfth grades. Students in these grades are commonly referred to as freshman (ninth grade), sophomore (tenth grade), junior (eleventh grade), and senior (twelfth grade). Students usually graduate from high school around the age of eighteen.

Students take a broad level and variety of classes with the intent to prepare them for higher education. There is usually not a set focus on a specific curriculum, and while students are required to take certain mandatory subjects, they may choose elective courses to complete their required class hours. Students are also allowed to participate in sports or music activities and study languages or many other subjects. High schools usually have "clubs" for after-school activities that are supervised by teachers or teaching assistants, such as foreign language clubs, clubs for the minor sports (and the school will usually have school teams for the major sports), film clubs, and other clubs that enrich the students and give them something to do until dinnertime at home.

Grades earned in high school are made available to colleges and universities in the form of a transcript when the student is applying to study. As a result, academic focus and good grades are critically important at this stage.

e. Higher education

Colleges and universities

After high school, young adults can continue their education in a two-year community or technical college or a four-year college or university. These are called "postsecondary institutions" or "institutions of higher education." There are public and private institutions of higher education. Public colleges and universities cost less than private ones, especially for residents of the state where the college or university is located. Young adults can also choose to attend schools to learn specific jobs, such as repairing computers or being a health-care assistant. Students in higher education choose a specific subject to study in depth (this subject is called their "major"). Choosing a major helps prepare them for employment or further education in that field.

A college or university education can be expensive. Some schools provide financial help called "scholarships." The US government also provides financial aid for students. Most students take out a loan or apply for financial aid or scholarships to help pay for their schooling. Certain scholarships and grants are limited to US citizens.

Federal financial aid for college students

The US government provides financial help to students attending certain institutions of higher education. This aid covers many school expenses, including tuition, fees, books, room and board, supplies, and transportation. Students qualify for this aid by their financial need, not their grades. There are three types of federal aid:

- grants—money that you don't have to repay
- work study—money that you earn while you are in school
- loans—money that you borrow that you must repay later with interest

For more information on federal financial aid programs, call (800) 433-3243 or visit the US Department of Education website www.studentaid.ed.gov/resources#funding. Information is also available in Spanish.

f. Postgraduate

Postgraduate education refers to education that prior to its pursuit requires at least a first (or bachelor's) degree to be eligible to enter the program. These include professional or academic certificates and usually start at the master's level.

The United States has many of the world's leading universities, offering postgraduate programs. The Fulbright Commission lists over seventeen hundred universities in the United States offering postgraduate degrees.

Acceptance into the top programs may be extremely competitive and generally requires a good undergraduate academic record, recommendations, and good scores on the relevant standardized test for the program (such as the GMAT to pursue an MBA, the GRE for most master's and PhD programs, the LSAT for the JD in law, and the MCAT for medical studies).

g. Adult education

Learning does not have to end when you become an adult. In the United States, people are encouraged to become lifelong learners. If you are sixteen years of age or older and have not completed high school, you can enroll in adult secondary education (ASE) classes. These classes prepare you to earn a General Educational Development (GED) certificate. A GED certificate is an alternative high school diploma.

It shows that you have learned high-school-level academic knowledge and skills. To earn a GED, you must take and pass tests in five different areas: reading, writing, social studies, science, and mathematics. Most US employers consider a GED credential to be equal to a regular high-school diploma. In many areas, GED preparation classes are free or low cost.

Chapter 5:

DOING BUSINESS IN THE UNITED STATES

The United States is considered one of the leading economies in which to do business or start a company. According to the World Bank, the United States is the fourth (as of the 2014 results) easiest place to do business in the world. When compared to other major economies, the United States is first. The comparisons are listed below:

Nation/Region	Rank
United States	4
United Kingdom	10
Canada	19
Germany	21
Japan	27
Regional average (OECD high income)	29
France	38
China	96

Source: *World Bank Doing Business 2014 Economy Profile: United States*

While on a comparative scale doing business in the United States is generally easy, there are some things that you will not be familiar with, and if you do not pay attention to them, they may cause some problems later.

The United States (at the federal, state, and local levels) has some very strict laws and rules covering employee treatment, overtime pay, insurance, collective bargaining, sexual harassment, taxes, and other items. When starting a new business it is always a good idea to speak with a qualified attorney to help you through this process.

a. Where to establish operations

Tips for choosing your business location

Choosing a business location is perhaps the most important decision a small-business owner or start-up will make, so it requires precise planning and research. It involves looking at demographics, assessing your supply chain, scoping the competition, staying on budget, understanding state laws and taxes, and much more.

Here are some tips to help you choose the right business location.

Determine your needs—Most businesses choose a location that provides exposure to customers. Additionally, there are less obvious factors and needs to consider:

- **Brand image**—Is the location consistent with the image you want to maintain?
- **Competition**—Are the businesses around you complementary or competing?
- **Local labor market**—Does the area have potential employees? What will their commute be like?
- **Plan for future growth**—If you anticipate further growth, look for a building that has extra space, should you need it.
- **Proximity to suppliers**—They need to be able to find you easily as well.
- **Safety**—Consider the crime rate. Will employees feel safe alone in the building or walking to their vehicles?
- **Zoning regulations**—These determine whether you can conduct your type of business in certain properties or locations. You can find out how property is zoned by contacting your local planning agency.

Evaluate your finances

Besides determining what you can afford, you will need to be aware of other financial considerations:

- **Hidden costs**—Very few spaces are business ready. Include costs like renovation, decorating, IT system upgrades, and so on.

- **Taxes**—What are the income and sales tax rates for your state? What about property taxes? Could you pay less in taxes by locating your business across a nearby state line?
- **Minimum wage**—While the federal minimum wage is $7.25 per hour, many states have a higher minimum. View the Department of Labor's list of minimum wage rates by state.
- **Government economic incentives**—Your business location can determine whether you qualify for government economic business programs, such as state-specific small business loans and other financial incentives.
- **Is the area business friendly?** - Understanding laws and regulations imposed on businesses in a particular location is essential. As you look to grow your business, it can be advantageous to work with a small-business specialist or counselor. Check what programs and support your state government and local community offer to small businesses. Many states offer online tools to help small-business owners start up and succeed. Local community resources such as SBA offices, Small Business Development Centers, Women's Business Centers, and other government-funded programs specifically support small businesses.
- **The bottom line**—Do your research. Talk to other business owners and potential co-tenants. Consult the small business community and utilize available resources, such as free government-provided demographic data, to help in your efforts.

b. Starting your own business

The business structure you choose will have legal and tax implications. Learn about the different types of business structures and find the one best suited for your business.

Sole proprietorship

A sole proprietorship is the simplest and most common structure chosen to start a business. It is an unincorporated business owned and run by one individual, with no distinction between the business and you, the owner. You are entitled to all profits and are responsible for all your business's debts, losses, and liabilities.

Forming a sole proprietorship

You do not have to take any formal action to form a sole proprietorship. As long as you are the only owner, this status automatically comes from your business activities. In fact, you may already own one without knowing it. If you are a freelance writer, for example, you are a sole proprietor.

But like all businesses, you need to obtain the necessary licenses and permits. Regulations vary by industry, state and locality. Use the licensing and permits tool offered by the SBA to find a listing of federal, state, and local permits, licenses, and registrations you'll need to run a business.

If you choose to operate under a name different than your own, you will most likely have to file a fictitious name, also known as an assumed name, trade name, or DBA name, short for "doing business as." You must choose an original name; it cannot already be claimed by another business.

Sole proprietor taxes

Because you and your business are one and the same, the business itself is not taxed separately—the sole proprietorship income is your income. You report income or losses and expenses with a Schedule C and the standard Form 1040. The bottom-line amount from Schedule C transfers to your personal tax return. It's your responsibility to withhold and pay all income taxes, including self-employment and estimated taxes. You can find more information about sole proprietorship taxes and other forms at IRS.gov.

Advantages of a sole proprietorship

Easy and inexpensive to form—A sole proprietorship is the simplest and least expensive business structure to establish. Costs are minimal, with legal costs limited to obtaining the necessary license or permits.

Complete control—Because you are the sole owner of the business, you have complete control over all decisions. You aren't required to consult with anyone else when you need to make decisions or want to make changes.

Easy tax preparation—Your business is not taxed separately, so it's easy to fulfill the tax reporting requirements for a sole proprietorship. The tax rates are also the lowest of the business structures.

Disadvantages of a proprietorship

Unlimited personal liability—Because there is no legal separation between you and your business, you can be held personally liable for the debts and obligations of the business. This risk extends to any liabilities incurred as a result of employee actions.

Hard to raise money—Sole proprietors often face challenges when trying to raise money. Because you can't sell stock in the business, investors won't often invest. Banks are also hesitant to lend to a sole proprietorship because of a perceived lack of credibility when it comes to repayment if the business fails.

Heavy burden—The flipside of complete control is the burden and pressure it can impose. You alone are ultimately responsible for the successes and failures of your business.

Limited-liability company

A limited-liability company is a hybrid type of legal structure that provides the limited-liability features of a corporation and the tax efficiencies and operational flexibility of a partnership.

The owners of an LLC are referred to as "members." Depending on the state, the members can consist of a single individual (one owner), two or more individuals, corporations, or other LLCs.

Unlike shareholders in a corporation, LLCs are not taxed as separate business entities. Instead, all profits and losses are passed through the business to each member of the LLC. LLC members report profits and losses on their personal federal tax returns, just as the owners of a partnership would.

Forming an LLC

While each state has slight variations to forming an LLC, they all adhere to some general principles.

Choose a business name. There are three rules that your LLC name needs to follow: (1) it must be different from an existing LLC in your state, (2) it must indicate that it's an LLC (such as LLC or Limited Company), and (3) it must not include words restricted by your state (such as "bank" and "insurance"). Your business name is automatically registered with your state when you register your business, so you do not have to go through a separate process. Read more here about choosing a business name.

File the articles of organization. The articles of organization is a simple document that legitimizes your LLC and includes information like your business name, address, and the names of its members. For most states, you file with the secretary of state. However, other states may require that you file with a different office such as the State Corporation Commission, Department of Commerce and Consumer Affairs, Department of Consumer and Regulatory Affairs, or the Division of Corporations & Commercial Code. Note: there may be an associated filing fee.

Create an operating agreement. Most states do not require operating agreements. However, an operating agreement is highly recommended for multimember LLCs, because it structures your LLC's finances and organization and provides rules and regulations for smooth operation. The operating agreement usually includes percentage of interests, allocation of profits and losses, members' rights and responsibilities, and other provisions.

Obtain licenses and permits. Once your business is registered, you must obtain business licenses and permits. Regulations vary by industry, state, and locality. You can use the SBA's licensing and permits tool to find a listing of federal, state, and local permits, licenses and registrations you'll need to run a business.

Hire employees. If you are hiring employees, read more about federal and state regulations for employers.

Announce your business. Some states, including Arizona and New York, require the extra step of publishing a statement in your local newspaper about your LLC formation. Check with your state's business filing office for requirements in your area.

LLC taxes

In the eyes of the federal government, an LLC is not a separate tax entity, so the business itself is not taxed. Instead, all federal income taxes are passed on to the LLC's members and are paid through their personal income tax. While the federal government does not tax income on an LLC, some states do, so check with your state's income tax agency.

Since the federal government does not recognize the LLC as a business entity for taxation purposes, all LLCs must file as a corporation, partnership, or sole proprietorship for tax purposes. Certain LLCs are automatically classified and taxed as a corporation by federal tax law. For guidelines about how to classify an LLC, visit IRS.gov.

LLCs that are not automatically classified as a corporation can choose their business entity classification. To elect a classification, an LLC must file Form 8832. This form is also used if an LLC wishes to change its classification status. Read more about filing as a corporation or partnership and filing as a single member LLC at IRS.gov.

You should file the following tax forms, depending on your classification:

- A single-member LLC files Form 1040 Schedule C like a sole proprietor.
- Partners in an LLC file a Form 1065 partnership tax return like owners in a traditional partnership.
- An LLC designated as a corporation files Form 1120, the corporation income tax return.

The IRS guide to limited-liability companies provides all relevant tax forms and additional information regarding their purpose and use.

Combining the benefits of an LLC with an S-Corp

There is always the possibility of requesting S-Corp status for your LLC. An attorney can advise you on the pros and cons. You'll have to make a special election with the IRS to have the LLC taxed as an S-Corp using Form 2553. You must file prior to the first two months and fifteen days of the beginning of the tax year in which the election is to take effect. For more information about S-Corp status, visit IRS.gov or read *Should My Company be an LLC, an S-Corp, or Both?*

The LLC remains a limited-liability company from a legal standpoint, but for tax purposes, it can be treated as an S-Corp. Be sure to contact the state's income tax agency where you plan to file your election form. Ask about the tax requirements and if they recognize elections of other entities (such as the S-Corp).

Advantages of an LLC

Limited liability—Members are protected from personal liability for business decisions or actions of the LLC. This means that if the LLC incurs debt or is sued, members' personal assets are usually exempt. This is similar to the liability protections afforded to shareholders of a corporation. Keep in mind that limited liability means "limited" liability—members are not necessarily shielded from wrongful acts, including those of their employees.

Less recordkeeping—An LLC's operational ease is one of its greatest advantages. Compared to an S corporation, there is less registration paper work, and there are smaller start-up costs.

Sharing of Profits. There are fewer restrictions on profit sharing within an LLC, as members distribute profits as they see fit. Members might contribute different proportions of capital and sweat equity. Consequently, it's up to the members themselves to decide who has earned what percentage of the profits or losses.

Disadvantages of an LLC

Limited life—In many states, when a member leaves an LLC, the business is dissolved, and the members must fulfill all remaining legal and business obligations to close the business. The remaining members can decide if they want to start a new LLC or part ways. However, you can include provisions in your operating agreement to prolong the life of the LLC if a member decides to leave the business.

Self-employment taxes—Members of an LLC are considered self-employed and must pay the self-employment tax contributions toward Medicare and Social Security. The entire net income of the LLC is subject to this tax.

Corporation (C Corporation)

A corporation (sometimes referred to as a C corporation) is an independent legal entity owned by shareholders. This means that the corporation itself, not the shareholders who own it, is held legally liable for the actions and debts the business incurs.

Corporations are more complex than other business structures, because they tend to have costly administrative fees, complex tax, and legal requirements. Because of these issues, corporations are generally suggested for established, larger companies with multiple employees.

For businesses in that position, corporations offer the ability to sell ownership shares in the business through stock offerings. "Going public" through an initial public offering (IPO) is a major selling point in attracting investment capital and high-quality employees.

Forming a corporation

A corporation is formed under the laws of the state in which it is registered. To form a corporation, you'll need to establish your business name and register your legal name with your state government. If you choose to operate under a name different from the officially registered name, you'll most likely have to file a fictitious name (also known as an assumed name, trade name, or DBA name, short for "doing business as"). State laws vary, but generally corporations must include a corporate designation (corporation, incorporated, limited) at the end of the business name.

To register your business as a corporation, you need to file certain documents, typically articles of incorporation, with your state's secretary of state office. Some states require corporations to establish directors and issue stock certificates to initial shareholders in the registration process. Contact your state business-entity registration office to find out about specific filing requirements in the state where you form your business.

Once your business is registered, you must obtain business licenses and permits. Regulations vary by industry, state and locality. Use our licensing and permits tool to find a listing of federal, state, and local permits, licenses, and registrations you'll need to run a business.

If you are hiring employees, read more about federal and state regulations for employers.

Corporation taxes

Corporations are required to pay federal, state and, in some cases, local taxes. Most businesses must register with the IRS, state, and local revenue agencies, and receive a tax ID number or permit.

When you form a corporation, you create a separate tax-paying entity. Regular corporations are called "C corporations" because subchapter C of chapter 1 of the Internal Revenue Code is where you find general tax rules affecting corporations and their shareholders.

Unlike sole proprietors and partnerships, corporations pay income tax on their profits. In some cases, corporations are taxed twice—first, when the company makes a profit, and again when dividends are paid to shareholders on their personal tax returns. Corporations use IRS Form 1120 or 1120-A, US corporation income tax return, to report revenue to the federal government.

Shareholders who are also employees pay income tax on their wages. The corporation and the employee each pay half of the Social Security and Medicare taxes, but this is usually a deductible business expense.

Read more about tax requirements for corporations on IRS.gov.

Advantages of a corporation

Limited liability—When it comes to taking responsibility for business debts and actions of a corporation, shareholders' personal assets are protected. Shareholders can generally only be held accountable for their investment in stock of the company.

Ability to generate capital—Corporations have an advantage when it comes to raising capital for their business: the ability to raise funds through the sale of stock.

Corporate tax treatment—Corporations file taxes separately from their owners. Owners of a corporation only pay taxes on corporate profits paid to them in the form of salaries, bonuses, and dividends, while any additional profits are awarded a corporate tax rate, which is usually lower than a personal income tax rate.

Attractive to potential employees—Corporations are generally able to attract and hire high-quality and motivated employees because they offer competitive benefits and the potential for partial ownership through stock options.

Disadvantages of a corporation

Time and money—Corporations are costly and time-consuming ventures to start and operate. Incorporating requires start-up, operating, and tax costs that most other structures do not require.

Double taxing—In some cases, corporations are taxed twice—first, when the company makes a profit, and again when dividends are paid to shareholders.

Additional paper work—Because corporations are highly regulated by federal, state and, in some cases, local agencies, there are increased paper-work and record-keeping burdens associated with this entity.

Partnership

A partnership is a single business where two or more people share ownership. Each partner contributes to all aspects of the business, including money, property, labor, or skill. In return, each partner shares in the profits and losses of the business.

Because partnerships entail more than one person in the decision-making process, it's important to discuss a wide variety of issues up front and develop a legal partnership agreement. This agreement should document how future business decisions will be made, including how the partners will divide profits, resolve disputes, and change ownership (bring in new partners or buy out current partners), and how to dissolve the partnership. Although partnership agreements are not legally required, they are strongly recommended, and it is considered extremely risky to operate without one.

Types of partnerships

General partnerships assume that profits, liability, and management duties are divided equally among partners. If you opt for an unequal distribution, the percentages assigned to each partner must be documented in the partnership agreement.

Limited partnerships (also known as a partnership with limited liability) are more complex than general partnerships. Limited partnerships allow partners to have limited liability as well as limited input with management decisions. These limits depend on the extent of each partner's investment percentage. Limited partnerships are attractive to investors of short-term projects.

Joint ventures act as general partnerships, but for only a limited period of time or for a single project. Partners in a joint venture can be recognized as an ongoing partnership if they continue the venture, but they must file as such.

Forming a partnership

To form a partnership, you must register your business with your state, a process generally done through your secretary of state's office.

You'll also need to establish your business name. For partnerships, your legal name is the name given in your partnership agreement or the last names of the partners. If you choose to operate under a name different than the officially registered name, you will most likely have to file a fictitious name (also known as an assumed name, trade name, or DBA name, short for "doing business as").

Once your business is registered, you must obtain business licenses and permits. Regulations vary by industry, state and locality. Use our licensing and permits tool to find a listing of federal, state, and local permits, licenses, and registrations you'll need to run a business.

If you are hiring employees, read more about federal and state regulations for employers.

Partnership taxes

Most businesses will need to register with the IRS, register with state and local revenue agencies, and obtain a tax ID number or permit.

A partnership must file an annual information return to report the income, deductions, gains, and losses from the business's operations, but the business itself does not pay income tax. Instead, the business passes through any profits or losses to its partners. Partners include their respective share of the partnership's income or loss on their personal tax returns.

Partnership taxes generally include

- annual return of income,
- employment taxes,
- excise taxes.

Partners in the partnership are responsible for several additional taxes, including

- income tax,
- self-employment tax,
- estimated tax.

Filing information for partnerships

- Partnerships must furnish copies of their Schedule K-1 (Form 1065) to all partners by the date Form 1065 is required to be filed, including extensions.
- Partners are not employees and should not be issued a Form W-2.
- The IRS guide to partnerships provides all relevant tax forms and additional information regarding their purpose and use.

Advantages of a partnership

Easy and inexpensive—A partnerships is generally an inexpensive and easily formed business structure. The majority of time spent starting a partnership often focuses on developing the partnership agreement.

Shared financial commitment—In a partnership, each partner is equally invested in the success of the business. Partnerships have the advantage of pooling resources to obtain capital. This could be beneficial in terms of securing credit or by simply doubling your seed money.

Complementary skills—A good partnership should reap the benefits of being able to utilize the strengths, resources, and expertise of each partner.

Partnership incentives for employees—Partnerships have an employment advantage over other entities if they offer employees the opportunity to become partners. Partnership incentives often attract highly motivated and qualified employees.

Disadvantages of a partnership

Joint and individual liability—Similar to sole proprietorships, partnerships retain full, shared liability among the owners. Partners are not only liable for their own actions but also for the business debts and decisions made by other partners. In addition, the personal assets of all partners can be used to satisfy the partnership's debt.

Disagreements among partners—With multiple partners, there are bound to be disagreements. Partners should consult each other on all decisions, make compromises, and resolve disputes as amicably as possible.

Shared profits—Because partnerships are jointly owned, each partner must share the successes and profits of their business with the other partners. An unequal contribution of time, effort, or resources can cause discord among partners.

S Corporations

An S corporation (sometimes referred to as an S-Corp) is a special type of corporation created through an IRS tax election. An eligible domestic corporation can avoid double taxation (once to the corporation and again to the shareholders) by electing to be treated as an S corporation.

An S-Corp is a corporation with the subchapter S designation from the IRS. To be considered an S-Corp, you must first charter a business as a corporation in the state where it is headquartered. According to the IRS, an S corporation is "considered by law to be a unique entity, separate and apart from those who own it." This limits the financial liability for which you (the owner or shareholder) are responsible. Nevertheless, liability protection is limited—S-Corps do not necessarily shield you from all litigation, such as an employee's tort actions as a result of a workplace incident.

What makes the S-Corp different from a traditional corporation (C-Corp) is that profits and losses can pass through to your personal tax return. Consequently, the business itself is not taxed. Only the shareholders are taxed. There is an important caveat, however: any shareholder who works for the company must pay him- or herself "reasonable compensation." Basically, the shareholder must be paid fair market value, or the IRS might reclassify any additional corporate earnings as wages.

Forming an S corporation

Before you form an S corporation, determine if your business will qualify under the IRS stipulations.

To file as an S corporation, you must first file as a corporation. After you are considered a corporation, all shareholders must sign and file Form 2553 to elect your corporation to become an S corporation.

Once your business is registered, you must obtain business licenses and permits. Regulations vary by industry, state, and locality. Use the licensing and permits tool to find a listing of federal, state, and local permits, licenses, and registrations you'll need to run a business.

If you are hiring employees, read more about federal and state regulations for employers.

Combining the benefits of an LLC with an S-Corp

There is always the possibility of requesting S-Corp status for your LLC. Your attorney can advise you on the pros and cons. You'll have to make a special election with the IRS to have the LLC taxed as an S-Corp using Form 2553. And you must file it before the first two months and fifteen days of the beginning of the tax year in which the election is to take effect.

The LLC remains a limited-liability company from a legal standpoint, but for tax purposes it's treated as an S-Corp. Be sure to contact your state's income tax agency, where you will file the election form, to learn about tax requirements.

Taxes

Most businesses need to register with the IRS, register with state and local revenue agencies, and obtain a tax ID number or permit.

Not all states tax S-Corps equally. Most recognize them similarly to the federal government and tax the shareholders accordingly. However, some states (like Massachusetts) tax S-Corps on profits above a specified limit. Other states don't recognize the S-Corp election and treat the business as a C-Corp with all of the tax ramifications. Some states (like New York and New Jersey) tax both the S-Corp's profits and the shareholders' proportional shares of the profits.

Your corporation must file the Form 2553 to elect S status within two months and fifteen days after the beginning of the tax year, or any time before the tax year, for the status to be in effect.

Advantages of an S corporation

Tax savings—One of the best features of the S-Corp is the tax savings for you and your business. While members of an LLC are subject to employment tax on the entire net income of the business, only the wages of the S-Corp shareholder who is an employee are subject to employment tax. The remaining income is paid to the owner as a "distribution," which is taxed at a lower rate, if at all.

Business expense tax credits—Some expenses that shareholder/employees incur can be written off as business expenses. Nevertheless, if such an employee owns 2 percent or more shares, then benefits like health and life insurance are deemed taxable income.

Independent life—An S-Corp designation also allows a business to have an independent life, separate from its shareholders. If a shareholder leaves the company or sells his or her shares, the S-Corp can continue doing business relatively undisturbed. Maintaining the business as a distinct corporate entity defines clear lines between the shareholders and the business that improve the protection of the shareholders.

Disadvantages of an S corporation

Stricter operational processes—As a separate structure, an S-Corp requires scheduled director and shareholder meetings, minutes from those meetings, adoption and updates to by-laws, stock transfers, and records maintenance.

Shareholder compensation requirements—A shareholder must receive reasonable compensation. The IRS takes notice of shareholder red flags like low salary/high distribution combinations and may reclassify your distributions as wages. You could pay a higher employment tax because of an audit with these results.

Choose your business name

Choosing a business name is an important step in the business planning process. Not only should you pick a name that reflects your brand identity, but you also need to ensure it is properly registered and protected for the long term. You should also give a thought to whether it's web-ready. Is the domain name even available?

Here are some tips to help you pick, register, and protect your business name.

Factors to consider when naming your business

Many businesses start out as freelancers, solo operations, or partnerships. In these cases, it's easy to fall back on your own name as your business name. While there's nothing wrong with this, it does make it tougher to present a professional image and build brand awareness.

Here are some points to consider as you choose a name:

- **How will your name look?**—Online, as part of a logo, on social media.
- **What connotations does it evoke?**—Is your name too corporate or not corporate enough? Does it reflect your business philosophy and culture? Does it appeal to your market?
- **Is it unique?**—Pick a name that hasn't been claimed by others, online or offline. A quick online search and domain name search (more on this below) will alert you to any existing use.
- **Check for trademarks**—Trademark infringement can carry a high cost for your business. Before you pick a name, use the US Patent and Trademark Office's trademark search tool to see if a similar name, or variations of it, is trademarked.

- **Check for existing businesses with the name**—If you intend to incorporate your business, you'll need to contact your state filing office to check whether your intended business name has already been claimed and is in use. If you find a business operating under your proposed name, you may still be able to use it, provided your business and the existing business offer different goods/services or are located in different regions.
- **Pick a name that is web-ready**—In order to claim a website address or URL, your business name needs to be unique and available. It should also be rich in key words that reflect what your business does. To find out if your business name has been claimed online, do a simple online search to see if anyone is already using that name. Next, check whether a domain name (or web address) is available. You can do this using the WHOIS database of domain names. If it is available, be sure to claim it right away. This guide explains how to register a domain name.
- **Claim your social media identity**—It's a good idea to claim your social media name early in the naming process—even if you are not sure which sites you intend to use. A name for your Facebook page can be set up and changed, but you can only claim a vanity URL or custom URL once you've got twenty-five fans or "likes." This custom URL name must be unique or unclaimed.

Apply for trademark protection

A trademark protects words, names, symbols, and logos that distinguish goods and services. Your name is one of your most valuable business assets, so it's worth protecting. You can file for a trademark for less than $300. Learn how to trademark your business name.

What is a "doing business as" name?

A fictitious name (or assumed name, trade name, or DBA name) is a business name that is different from your personal name, the names of your partners, and the officially registered name of your LLC or corporation.

It's important to note that when you form a business, the legal name of the business defaults to the name of the person or entity that owns the business, unless you choose to rename it and register it as a DBA name.

For example, consider this scenario: John Smith sets up a painting business. Rather than operate under his own name, John instead chooses to name his business "John Smith Painting." This name is considered an assumed name, and John will need to register it with the appropriate local-government agency.

The legal name of your business is required on all government forms and applications, including your application for employer tax IDs, licenses, and permits.

Do I need a "doing business as" name? A DBA is needed in the following scenarios:

- **Sole proprietors or partnerships**—If you wish to start a business under anything other than your real name, you'll need to register a DBA so that you can do business as another name.
- **Existing corporations or LLCs**—If your business is already set up, and you want to do business under a name other than your existing corporation or LLC name, you will need to register a DBA.

Note: Not all states require the registering of fictitious business names or DBAs.

Register your DBA with your county clerk's office or with your state government, depending on where your business is located. There are a few states that do not require the registering of fictitious business names.

Register your business with state agencies

Some business types require registration with your state government:

- a corporation
- a nonprofit organization
- a limited-liability company or partnership

If you establish your business as a sole proprietorship, there is no need to register it at the state level. However, many states require sole proprietors to use their own name for the business name unless they formally file another name. This is known as your doing-business-as (DBA) name, trade name, or fictitious name.

Select a state to find out about specific filing requirements in the state where you will form your business.

c. Buying an existing business

For some entrepreneurs, buying an existing business represents less of a risk than starting a new business from scratch. While the opportunity may be less risky in some aspects, you must perform due diligence to ensure that you are fully aware of the terms of the purchase.

If you have decided to buy an existing business, you will want to be sure you are making the right choice in your new venture. Only you can determine the right business for your needs; however, the following topics can help guide you make the best decision.

The steps to starting

There are many different types of businesses to buy. Take these steps to narrow down the list of potential businesses you may want to purchase.

Identify your interests. If you have absolutely no idea what business you want to invest in, first eliminate businesses that are of no interest to you.

Consider your talents. Being honest about your skills and experience can help you eliminate unrealistic business ventures.

List conditions for your business. Consider if a business has a condition that is unfavorable to you, such as location and time commitment.

Quantify your investment. Finding profitable businesses for sale at reasonable prices can be difficult. Ask yourself why this business is for sale in the first place.

Advantages to choosing an existing business

There are many favorable aspects to buying an existing business, such as drastic reduction in start-up costs. You may be able to jump-start your cash flow immediately because of existing inventory and receivables.

Disadvantages to choosing an existing business

There are also some downsides to buying an existing business. Purchasing cost may be much higher than the cost of starting a new business because of the initial business concept, customer base, brand, and other fundamental work that has already been done. Also, be aware of hidden problems associated with the business, such as debts the business is owed that you may not be able to collect.

Doing due diligence

As you become a business owner, there are items that need to be addressed before entering into any business agreements or transactions.

Obtain all licenses and permits. Most businesses need licenses and permits to operate. The type of license or permit you need depends on your industry and the state in which the business is located. Use SBA's licenses and permits finder tool to get a listing of federal, state, and local permits and licenses you will need to run your business.

Check zoning requirements. Zoning requirements may affect the type of business that you are intending to operate in a particular area. Visit the SBA's basic zoning laws page for more information about zoning and to ensure that your business is abiding by all laws in your area.

Check environmental concerns. If you are acquiring real property along with the business, it is important to check the environmental regulations in the area. Visit EPA's small business gateway page for more information.

Determining the value of a business

There are a number of different methods to determine a fair and equitable price for the sale of the business. Here are a few:

- **Capitalized earning approach**—This method refers to the return on the investment that is expected by an investor.
- **Excess earning method**—This is similar to the capitalized earning method, except that it separates return on assets from other earnings.
- **Cash flow method**—This method is typically used when attempting to determine how much of a loan the cash flow of the business will support. The adjusted cash flow is used as a benchmark to measure the firm's ability to service debt.
- **Tangible assets (balance sheet) method**—This method values the business by the tangible assets.
- **Value of specific intangible assets method**—This method compares buying a wanted intangible asset versus creating it.

For more information, read SCORE's article "How to Value Your Business."

Doing research for purchasing a business

Once you have found a business that you would like to buy, it is important to conduct a thorough, objective investigation. The following list includes important information you want to include when researching the business you want to buy:

- **Letter of intent**—The letter of intent should spell out the proposed price, the terms of the purchase, and the conditions for the sale of the business.
- **Confidentiality agreement**—A confidentiality agreement indicates that you will not use the information about the seller's business for any purpose other than making the decision to buy it.
- **Contracts and leases**—If the business has a current lease for the location, be aware that you may have to work with the landlord to assume any existing lease on the business premises or negotiate a new lease.

- **Financial statements**—Examine the financial statements from the business for at least the past three to five years. Also make sure that an audit letter from a reputable CPA firm accompanies the statements. You should not accept a simple financial review by the business itself.
- **Tax returns**—Review the business's tax returns from the past three to five years. This will help you determine the profitability of the business as well as any outstanding tax liability.
- **Important documents**—Numerous documents should be checked during your investigation. Examples include property documents, customer lists, sales records, advertising materials, employee and manager information, and contracts.
- **Professional help**—A qualified attorney should be enlisted to help review the legal and organizational documents of the business you are planning to purchase. In addition, an accountant can help with a thorough evaluation of the financial condition of the business.

Sales agreement for buying a business

The sales agreement is the key document to finalize the purchase of the business. This agreement defines everything that you intend to purchase, including business assets, customer lists, intellectual property, and goodwill. If you do not have a lawyer to help you draft the terms of the sale, you should at least have one review the agreement before you sign it.

Checklist for closing on a business

The closing is the final step in the process of buying a business. Keep in mind that you should have legal counsel available to review all documentation necessary for the transfer of the business. The following items should be addressed in a closing:

- **Adjusted purchase price**—This will include prorated items such as rent, utilities, and inventory up to the time of closing.
- **Review required documents**—These documents should include a corporate resolution approving the sale, evidence that the corporation is in good standing, or any tax releases that may have been promised by the seller. Check with your local department of corporations or secretary of state for more information.
- **Signed promissory note**—In some cases, the seller will have back financing, so have an attorney review any documentation.

- **Security agreements**—A security agreement lists the assets that will be used for security as a promise for payment of the loan.

Uniform Commercial Code (UCC) financing statements are recorded with the secretary of state in the state you will be purchasing your business.

- **Lease**—If you agree to take over the lease, make sure that you have the landlord's concurrence. If you are negotiating a new lease with the landlord instead of assuming the existing lease, make sure both parties are in agreement of the terms of the new lease.
- **Vehicles**—If the purchase of the business includes vehicles, you may have to complete transfer documents for the vehicles. Check with your local Department of Motor Vehicles to determine the correct procedure and necessary forms.
- **Bill of sale**—The bill of sale proves the sale of the business. It also explicitly transfers ownership of tangible business assets not specifically transferred on their own.
- **Patents, trademarks, and copyrights**—If there are any patents, trademarks, or copyrights associated with the business, you may need to complete the necessary forms as part of the transaction.
- **Franchise**—You may need to complete franchise documents if the business is a franchise. See the "Consumer Guide to Buying a Franchise" (http://www.sba.gov/content/consumer-guide-buying-franchise) for more information.
- **Closing or settlement sheet:** The closing or settlement sheet will list all financial aspects of the transaction. Everything listed on the settlement should have been negotiated prior to the closing.

Covenant not to compete—It is a good idea to have the seller sign an agreement to not compete against the business. This will help prevent any interference from the previous owner.

Consultation/employment agreement—If the seller is agreeing to remain on for a specified amount of time, this documentation is necessary for legal purposes.

IRS Form 8594 asset acquisition statement—This document will indicate how the purchase was allocated and the amount of assets, which are important for your tax return.

Bulk sale laws—Make sure that you comply with bulk sale laws, which govern the sale of business inventory.

Hiring your first employee

If your business is booming, but you are struggling to keep up, perhaps it's time to hire some help. The eight steps below can help you start the hiring process and ensure you are compliant with key federal and state regulations.

Step 1. Obtain an employer identification number (EIN). Before hiring your first employee, you need to get an employment identification number (EIN) from the US Internal Revenue Service. The EIN is often referred to as an employer tax ID or as Form SS-4. The EIN is necessary for reporting taxes and other documents to the IRS. In addition, the EIN is necessary when reporting information about your employees to state agencies. Apply for EIN online or contact the IRS at (800) 829-4933.

Step 2. Set up records for withholding taxes. According to the IRS, you must keep records of employment taxes for at least four years. Keeping good records can also help you monitor the progress of your business, prepare financial statements, identify sources of receipts, keep track of deductible expenses, prepare your tax returns, and support items reported on tax returns.

Below are three types of withholding taxes you need for your business:

Federal income tax withholding—Every employee must provide an employer with a signed withholding exemption certificate (Form W-4) on or before the date of employment. The employer must then submit Form W-4 to the IRS.

Federal wage and tax statement—Every year, employers must report to the federal government wages paid and taxes withheld for each employee. This report is filed using Form W-2, wage and tax statement. Employers must complete a W-2 form for each employee to whom they pay a salary, wage, or other compensation.

Employers must send Copy A of W-2 forms to the Social Security Administration by the last day of February to report wages and taxes of your employees for the previous calendar year. In addition, employers should send copies of W-2 forms to their employees by January 31 of the year following the reporting period. Visit SSA.gov/employer for more information.

State taxes—Depending on the state where your employees are located, you may be required to withhold state income taxes. Visit the state and local tax page for more information.

Step 3. Verify employee eligibility. Federal law requires employers to verify an employee's eligibility to work in the United States. Within three days of hire, employers must complete Form I-9, employment eligibility verification, which requires employers to examine documents to confirm the employee's citizenship or eligibility to work in the United States. Employers can only request documentation specified on the I-9 form.

Employers do not need to submit the I-9 form to the federal government but are required to keep them on file for three years after the date of hire or one year after the date of the employee's termination, whichever is later.

Employers can use information taken from the Form I-9 to electronically verify the employment eligibility of newly hired employees by registering with E-Verify (http://www.uscis.gov/e-verify).

Visit the US Immigration and Customs Enforcement agency's I-9 website to download the form and find more information.

Step 4. Register with your state's New Hire Reporting Program. All employers are required to report newly hired and rehired employees to a state directory within twenty days of their hire or rehire date. Visit the new hires reporting requirements page (http://www.sba.gov/content/new-hire-reporting-your-state) to learn more and find links to your state's New Hire Reporting system.

Step 5. Obtain workers' compensation insurance. All businesses with employees are required to carry workers' compensation insurance coverage through a commercial carrier, on a self-insured basis, or through their state's workers' compensation insurance program.

Step 6. Post required notices. Employers are required to display certain posters in the workplace that inform employees of their rights and employer responsibilities under labor laws. Visit the "Workplace Posters" (http://www.sba.gov/content/posters) page for specific federal and state posters you'll need for your business.

Step 7. File your taxes. Generally, employers who pay wages subject to income tax withholding, Social Security, and Medicare taxes must file IRS Form 941, Employer's Quarterly Federal Tax Return. For more information, visit IRS.gov.

New and existing employers should consult the IRS "Employer's Tax Guide" to understand all their federal tax filing requirements.

Visit the state and local tax pages for specific tax filing requirements for employers.

Step 8. Get organized and keep yourself informed. Being a good employer doesn't stop with fulfilling your various tax and reporting obligations. Maintaining a healthy and fair workplace, providing benefits, and keeping employees informed about your company's policies are key to your business's success.

Here are some additional steps you should take after you've hired your first employee:

Set up record keeping

In addition to requirements for keeping payroll records of your employees for tax purposes, certain federal employment laws also require you to keep records about your employees. The following sites provide more information about federal reporting requirements:

- Tax Record-Keeping Guidance:
  http://www.sba.gov/content/learn-about-your-state-and-local-tax-obligations
- Labor Record-Keeping Requirements:
  http://www.irs.gov/businesses/small/article/0,,id=98575,00.html
- Occupational Safety and Health Act Compliance:
  http://www.osha.gov/dcsp/compliance_assistance/quickstarts/index.html
- Employment Law Guide (employee benefits chapter):
  http://www.dol.gov/compliance/guide/erisa.htm
- Managing Employees:
  http://www.sba.gov/content/managing-employees

Complying with standards for employee rights in regards to equal opportunity and fair labor standards is a requirement. Following statutes and regulations for minimum wage, overtime, and child labor will help you avoid error and a lawsuit. See the Department of Labor's Employment Law Guide (http://www.dol.gov/compliance/guide/) for up-to-date information on these statutes and regulations.

There's a lot more to being an employer than hiring staff. To protect your business and your workers, employers must have a solid understanding of federal and state labor laws. We've written many articles on the various topics related to human resource management, and here is a quick overview of Business.gov's employment, labor law, and benefit information, covering everything from wages to discrimination.

Hiring and terminating employees

Good HR skills can make hiring a new employee a painless process or, if done incorrectly, a difficult one. In addition to finding, interviewing, and selecting the right workers, employers must comply with a wide variety of employment laws. Similarly, just as hiring and managing employees involves several legal steps, so does firing or laying off employees.For more information, check out Business.gov's guides to hiring employees and contractors and terminating employees. These brief articles will also help you to learn more about your responsibilities as an employer:

- 10 Regulatory Steps You Must Follow When Hiring Your First Employee
  http://www.sba.gov/content/10-steps-hiring-your-first-employee

- 5 Things to Know About Hiring Independent Contractors
  http://www.sba.gov/community/blogs/community-blogs/business-law-advisor/5-things-know-about-hiring-independent-contractors
- Handling Employee Layoffs as a Small Business Owner
  http://www.sba.gov/community/blogs/community-blogs/small-business-matters/handling-employee-layoffs-small-business-owner

Benefits and compensation

It's important for employers to know what they are required by law to provide, what benefits are considered optional, and what industry standards are. Without a good plan and package, you are unlikely to get the quality of employee that you desire. For more information on the steps to take to comply with mandatory regulations and tips on setting up an employee benefits plan, check out Business.gov's guides to employee benefits and wage and hour laws, and the following brief articles:

- Employee Benefit Plans: What's Law and What's Optional
  http://www.sba.gov/community/blogs/community-blogs/small-business-matters/employee-benefit-plans-whats-law-and-whats-optional
- Finding and Managing the Right Retirement Plan for Your Small Business
  http://www.sba.gov/community/blogs/community-blogs/small-business-matters/finding-and-managing-right-retirement-plan-your-small-business
- I'm Hungry: Aren't Lunch Breaks Required?
  http://www.sba.gov/community/blogs/community-blogs/business-law-advisor/im-hungry-arent-lunch-breaks-required
- Paying the Boss: 4 Tips for Setting Your Own Salary
  http://www.sba.gov/community/blogs/community-blogs/small-business-cents/paying-boss-4-tips-setting-your-own-salary

Disability and workplace safety

Employers are responsible for establishing and maintaining a healthy workplace environment for their employees. While every business should ensure that safety policies are in place to prevent workplace accidents, disability and workers' compensation policies ensure that medical treatment, vocational rehabilitation, and other benefits are available if employees are hurt on the job. For more information, check out Business.gov's guides to Workplace Safety and Health (http://www.sba.gov/content/workplace-safety-health) and Workers' Compensation (http://www.sba.gov/content/workers-compensation), and these brief articles on federal and state requirements that apply to your business:

- Ensuring a Healthy and Risk-Free Workplace
- Free Workplace Safety Handbook for Small Businesses
- Hurt on the Job: An Employer's Action Plan for Workplace Injuries

Discrimination and harassment

Although some employers may never encounter these issues, discrimination and harassment in the workplace is a serious subject and must be handled carefully. As an employer, it's important to understand discrimination laws and to teach and train your employees on their rights and responsibilities. Being proactive about these policies is an employer's best tool in creating an appropriate and comfortable workplace. For more information, check out Business.gov's guide to Employment Discrimination and Harassment (http://www.sba.gov/content/employment-discrimination-and-harassment), and these brief articles that govern workplace behavior:

- Age Discrimination Act: FAQs for Small Business Owners
  http://www.sba.gov/blogs/age-discrimination-act-faqs-small-business-owners
- Employer's Guide to Discrimination: Hiring and Managing Employees with Criminal Records
  http://www.sba.gov/community/blogs/community-blogs/business-law-advisor/employers-guide-discrimination-hiring-and-man-0
- Employer's Guide to Discrimination: Fair Wages and The Equal Pay Act
  http://www.sba.gov/community/blogs/community-blogs/business-law-advisor/employers-guide-discrimination-fair-wages-and-e
- Employer's Guide to Discrimination: Pregnancy Discrimination
  http://www.sba.gov/community/blogs/community-blogs/business-law-advisor/employers-guide-discrimination-pregnancy-discri
- Sexual Harassment in the Workplace—Forming a Basis for Prevention and Management
  http://www.sba.gov/community/blogs/community-blogs/small-business-matters/sexual-harassment-workplace-forming-basis-pre

Hire a contractor or an employee?

Independent contractors and employees are not the same, and it is important to understand the difference. Knowing this distinction will help you determine what your first hiring move will be, affect how you withhold a variety of taxes, and help you avoid costly legal consequences.

What is the difference?

An independent contractor

- operates under a business name,
- has his/her own employees,
- maintains a separate business checking account,
- advertises his/her business's services,
- invoices for work completed,
- has more than one client,
- has own tools and sets own hours,
- keeps business records.

An employee

- performs duties dictated or controlled by others,
- is given training for work to be done,
- works for only one employer.

Many small businesses rely on independent contractors for their staffing needs. There are many benefits to using contractors over hiring employees:

- savings in labor costs
- reduced liability
- flexibility in hiring and firing

Why does it matter?

Misclassification of individuals as an independent contractor may have a number of costly legal consequences. If your independent contractors meet the legal definition of employee, you may be required to:

- reimburse them for wages you should have paid them under the Fair Labor Standards Act, including overtime and minimum wage;
- pay back taxes and penalties for federal and state income taxes, Social Security, Medicare, and unemployment;
- pay any misclassified injured employees' workers' compensation benefits;
- Provide employee benefits, including health insurance, retirement, etc.

Tax requirements

Visit the IRS Independent Contractor or Employee guide (http://www.irs.gov/Businesses/Small-Businesses-&-Self-Employed/Independent-Contractor-Self-Employed-or-Employee) to learn about the tax implications of either scenario, download and fill out a form to have the IRS officially determine your workers' status, and find other related resources.

Employment information

There is no single test for determining if an individual is an independent contractor or an employee under the Fair Labor Standards Act. However, the following guidelines should be taken into account:

- the extent to which the services rendered are an integral part of the principal's business
- the permanency of the relationship
- the amount of the alleged contractor's investment in facilities and equipment
- the nature and degree of control by the principal
- the alleged contractor's opportunities for profit and loss
- the amount of initiative, judgment, or foresight in open market competition with others that is required for the success of the claimed independent contractor
- the degree of independent business organization and operation

Whether a person is an independent contractor or an employee generally depends on the amount of control exercised by the employer over the work being done. Read *Equal Employment Opportunity Laws—Who's Covered?* (http://www.eeoc.gov/policy/docs/threshold.html#2-III-A) for more information on how to determine whether a person is an independent contractor or an employee and which are covered under federal laws.

d. Business banking and finance

i) Estimating start-up costs

If you are planning to start a business, it is critical to determine your budgetary needs.

Different businesses have different needs. Some businesses run on a smaller budget, while others may require considerable investment in inventory or equipment. Additional considerations may include the cost to acquire or renovate a building, or the purchase of long-term equipment.

To determine how much seed money you need to start, you must estimate the costs of doing business for the first months. Some of these expenses will be one-time costs, such as the fee for incorporating your business or the price of a sign for your building. Some will be ongoing costs, such as the cost of utilities, inventory, insurance, etc.

While identifying these costs, decide whether they are essential or optional. A realistic start-up budget should only include those things that are necessary to start a business.

These essential expenses can be fixed or variable. Fixed expenses include rent, utilities, administrative costs, and insurance costs. Variable expenses include inventory, shipping and packaging costs, sales commissions, and other costs associated with the direct sale of a product or service. The most effective way to calculate your start-up costs is to use a worksheet that lists both one-time and ongoing costs.

Finance your business
Borrowing money for your business

After you have developed a cash flow analysis and determined when your business will make profit, you may decide you need additional funding. Borrowing money is one of the most common sources of funding for a small business, but obtaining a loan isn't always easy. Before you approach a lender for a loan, you will need to understand the factors the bank will use to evaluate your application. This section outlines some of the key factors a lender uses to analyze a potential borrower.

Types of financing

There are two types of financing: equity financing and debt financing. When looking for money, you must consider your company's debt-to-equity ratio (the relation between dollars you have borrowed and dollars you have invested in your business.) The more money owners have invested in their business, the easier it is to obtain financing.

If your firm has a high ratio of equity to debt, you should probably seek debt financing. However, if your company has a high proportion of debt to equity, experts advise that you should increase your ownership capital (equity investment) for additional funds. This will prevent you from being overleveraged to the point of jeopardizing your company's survival.

a. Equity financing

Equity financing (or equity capital) is money raised by a company in exchange for a share of ownership in the business. Ownership accounts for owning shares of stock outright or having the right to convert other financial instruments into stock. It allows a business to obtain funds without incurring debt, or without having to repay a specific amount of money at a particular time.

Most small or growth-stage businesses use limited equity financing. Equity often comes from investors such as friends, relatives, employees, customers, or industry colleagues, though it mostly comes from venture capitalists. These are institutional risk takers and may be groups of wealthy individuals, government-assisted sources, or major financial institutions. Most specialize in one or a few closely related industries.

b. Debt financing

Debt financing means borrowing money that must be repaid over a period of time, usually with interest. Debt financing can be either short-term, with full repayment due in less than one year, or long-term, with repayment due over a period greater than one year. The lender does not gain an ownership interest in the business, and debt obligations are typically limited to repaying the loan with interest. Loans are often secured by some or all of the assets of the company. In addition, lenders commonly require the borrower's personal guarantee in case of default. This ensures that the borrower has a sufficient personal interest at stake in the business.

Loans can be obtained from sources such as banks, savings and loans institutions, credit unions, and commercial finance companies. There are also SBA-guaranteed loans. State and local governments have many programs that encourage the growth of small businesses. Family members, friends, and former associates are all potential sources, especially when capital requirements are smaller.

Traditionally, banks have been the major source of small business funding. The principal roles of banks include short-term loans, seasonal lines of credit, and single-purpose loans for machinery and equipment. Banks generally have been reluctant to offer long-term loans to small firms. SBA's guaranteed lending programs encourage banks and nonbank lenders to make long-term loans to small firms by reducing their risk and leveraging the funds they have available.

Ability to repay

The ability (or capacity) to repay the funds you receive from a lender must be justified in your loan package. Banks want to see two sources of repayment—cash flow from the business and a secondary source, such as collateral. The lender reviews the past financial statements of a business to analyze its cash flow.

Generally, banks are more comfortable offering assistance to businesses that have been in existence for a number of years and have a proven financial track record. If the business has consistently made a profit, and that profit can cover the payment of additional debt, it is likely that the loan will be approved. If however, the business is a start-up or has been operating marginally and has an opportunity to grow, it is necessary to prepare a thorough loan package with a detailed explanation that includes how the business will be able to repay the loan.

a. *Credit history*

When a small business requests a loan, one of the first things a lender looks at is personal and business credit history. So before you even start the process of preparing a loan request, you want to make sure you have good credit.

Get your personal credit report from one of the credit bureaus, such as TransUnion, Equifax, or Experian. You should initiate this step well in advance of seeking a loan. Personal credit reports may contain errors or be out of date, and it can take three to four weeks for errors to be corrected. It is up to you to see that corrections are made, so make sure you check regularly on progress. You want to make sure that when a lender pulls your credit report, all the errors have been corrected, and your history is up to date.

Once you obtain your credit report, check to make sure that all personal information—including your name, Social Security number, and address—is correct. Then carefully examine the rest of the report, which contains a list of all the credit you obtained in the past, such as credit cards, mortgages, and student loans, and information on how you paid that credit. Any item indicating that you have had a problem in paying on time will be toward the top of the list. These past payments may affect your ability to obtain a loan.

A person may have a period of bad credit as a result of divorce, medical crisis, or some other significant event. If you can show that your credit was good before and after this event and that you have tried to pay back those debts, you should be able to obtain a loan. It is best if you write an explanation of your credit problems and how you have rectified them, and attach this to your credit report in your loan package.

Each credit bureau has a slightly different way of presenting your credit information. Contact the bureau you used for more specific information on how to read your credit report. If you need additional help in interpreting or evaluating your credit report, ask your accountant or a local banker.

b. Equity investment

Don't be misled into thinking that a start-up business can obtain all financing through conventional or special loan programs. Financial institutions want to see a certain amount of equity in a business.

Equity can be built up through retained earnings or by the injection of cash from either the owner or investors. Most banks want to see that the total liabilities or debt of a business is not more than four times the amount of equity, so if you want a loan for your business, make sure that there is enough equity in the company to leverage that loan.

Owners usually must put some of their own money into the business to get a loan. The amount of financing depends on the type of loan, purpose, and terms. Most banks want the owner to put in at least 20–40 percent of the total request.

Having the right debt-to-equity ratio does not guarantee your business will get a loan. There are a number of other factors used to evaluate a business, such as net worth—the amount of equity in a business—which is often a combination of retained earnings and owner's equity.

c. Collateral

When a financial institution gives a loan, it wants to make sure it will get its money back. That is why a lender usually requires a second source of repayment, called collateral. Collateral is personal and business assets that can be sold in case the cash generated by the small business is not sufficient to repay the loan. Every loan program requires at least some collateral. If a potential borrower has no collateral, he/she will need a cosigner who has collateral to pledge. Otherwise, it may be difficult to obtain a loan.

The value of collateral is not based on market value; rather, it is discounted to take into account the value that would be lost if the assets had to be liquidated.

d. Collateral coverage ratio

bank will calculate your collateral coverage ratio as part of the loan evaluation process. This ratio is calculated by dividing the total discounted collateral value by the total loan request.

e. Management experience

Managerial expertise is a critical element in the success of any business. In fact, poor management is most frequently cited as the reason businesses fail. Lenders will be looking closely at your education and experience as well as that of your key managers.

f. Questions your lender will ask

Before you apply for a loan, you need to think about a variety of questions:

- Can the business repay the loan? (Is cash flow greater than debt service?)
- Can you repay the loan if the business fails? (Is collateral sufficient to repay the loan?)
- Does the business collect its bills?
- Does the business pay its bills?
- Does the business control its inventory?
- Does the business control expenses?
- Are the officers committed to the business?
- Does the business have a profitable operating history?
- Does the business match its sources and uses of funds?
- Are sales growing?
- Are profits increasing as a percentage of sales?
- Is there any discretionary cash flow?
- What is the future of the industry?
- Who is your competition, and what are their strengths and weaknesses?

e. Permits and licenses

This section gives an overview of city, state, and federal systems and how to look these things up.

Federal licenses and permits

If your business is involved in activities supervised and regulated by a federal agency—such as selling alcohol, firearms, commercial fishing, etc.—then you may need to obtain a federal license or permit. Here follows a brief list of business activities that require these forms and information on how to apply.

In addition, you can also use SBA's Permit Me (http://www.sba.gov/licenses-and-permits) search tool to find general business permits, licenses and registrations required by your state, county, or city.

Agriculture

If you import or transport animals, animal products, biologics, biotechnology, or plants across state lines, you'll need to apply for a permit from the US Department of Agriculture (USDA).

Alcoholic beverages

If you manufacture, wholesale, import, or sell alcoholic beverages at a retail location, you will need to register your business and obtain certain federal permits (for tax purposes) with the US Treasury's Alcohol and Tobacco Tax and Trade Bureau (TTB) (http://www.ttb.gov/index.shtml). The website has a number of online tools that make this process straightforward. If you are just starting a business in this trade, start by reading the TTB's New Visitors Guide which offers helpful information for small-business owners.

Remember, you will also need to contact your local Alcohol Beverage Control Board for local alcohol business permit and licensing information.

Aviation

Does your business involve the operation of aircraft, the transportation of goods or people via air, or aircraft maintenance? If so, you'll need to apply for one or more of the following licenses and certificates from the Federal Aviation Administration:

- FAA Licenses and Certificates (http://www.faa.gov/licenses_certificates/) —Get licensing information for airmen, aircraft, airports, airlines, and medical aviation services.
- Pilot Licenses and Training Requirements (http://www.faa.gov/pilots/)
- Aircraft Mechanic Licenses

Firearms, ammunition, and explosives

Businesses that manufacture, deal in, or import firearms, ammunition, and explosives must comply with the Gun Control Act's licensing requirements. The act is administered by the Bureau of Alcohol, Tobacco, Firearms and Explosives (ATF) (http://www.atf.gov/). Refer to the following resources from the ATF to make sure your business is properly licensed:

- *Firearms Industry Guide* (http://www.atf.gov/firearms/industry/)—Includes information on obtaining and renewing a federal firearms license, importing firearms and ammunitions, and more.
- *Explosives Industry Guide* (http://www.atf.gov/explosives/industry/) — Find out how to get a federal explosives license.
- *How to Become a Federal Firearms Licensee (FFL)* (http://www.atf.gov/firearms/how-to/)
- *How to Become a Federal Explosives Licensee (FEL)* (http://www.atf.gov/explosives/how-to/become-an-fel.html)

Mining and drilling

Businesses involved in drilling for natural gas, oil or other mineral resources on federal lands may be required to obtain a drilling permit from the Bureau of Ocean Energy Management, Regulation, and Enforcement (formerly the Minerals Management Service).

Nuclear energy

Producers of commercial nuclear energy and fuel cycle facilities, as well as businesses involved in the distribution and disposal of nuclear materials, must apply for a license from the US Nuclear Regulatory Commission.

Radio and television broadcasting

If your business broadcasts information by radio, television, wire, satellite, or cable, you may be required to obtain a license from the Federal Communications Commission (FCC).

Transportation and logistics

If you operate an oversize or overweight vehicle, you'll need to abide by the US Department of Transportation guidelines on maximum weight. Permits for oversize/overweight vehicles are issued by your state government.

State licenses and permits

Starting a business? Confused about whether you need a business license or permit?

Virtually every business needs some form of license or permit to operate legally. However, licensing and permit requirements vary, depending on the type of business you are operating, where it's located, and what government rules apply.

To help you identify the specific licenses or permits your business may need, use SBA.gov's Permit Me tool. Simply enter your zip code and business type to view a list of the licenses or permits you'll need, together with information and links to the application process.

Chapter 6:

TAXES

a. Individual

US taxpayers are required to report and pay taxes in the United States on their worldwide income, regardless of where it was earned, where they lived, and even if they already paid taxes to another country. In general these types of income include compensation income, interests, dividends, and other investment income, business income, capital gains, rental income, and pension income.

A lawful permanent resident ("LPR") becomes a US resident and US taxpayer when he or she receives the alien registration card (or green card) for immigration purposes. Tax residency begins in the year, and in most cases on the first day, that the LPR is present in the United States, and the first day of the year following the receipt of the green card regardless of whether the LPR ever comes to the United States.

Residency then continues until (a) the LPR status has been revoked, (b) it has been administratively or judicially determined to have been abandoned, or (c) the US residence status is affected by an international tax treaty whereby the LPR is not subject to double taxation.

Once residency has been established, it is irrelevant if the LPR remains present in the United States and he or she will remain subject to all of the same tax rules applicable to US citizens unless he or she loses the LPR status.

Reporting obligations

While the scope of this presentation is not large enough to encompass all of the potential reporting obligations of a US taxpayer, below you will find some common examples of reporting obligations for resident aliens:

- You are required to report your worldwide income annually. This includes income (for example dividends, rents, foreign currency, or interest) that is received and kept offshore. This is generally done on IRS form 1040 US Individual Income Tax Return.
- You are required to report all of your offshore financial accounts to the US Treasury on an annual basis if the aggregate value exceeds $10,000 at any time during the year. These include those beneficially owned by you in any way, and also accounts to which you are a signatory (such as business and trust accounts). This is done on Treasury Department Form TD F 90-22.1.
- You are required to report beneficial ownership of specified foreign financial assets that includes any financial account, stock, or securities issued by someone who is not a US person, any interest in a foreign entity, any financial instrument or contract with an issuer or counterparty that is not a US person. This obligation begins when (if filing single or separately) the foreign financial assets exceeds (1) $50,000 on the last day of the year, or (2) $75,000 on any day during the tax year; for married couples the threshold is (1) $100,000 on the last day of the tax year, or (2) $150,000 on any day during the tax year. This is done in IRS Form 8938, Statement of Specified Foreign Financial Assets.

Tax rates in general (individual)

In the United States, income tax is imposed by the federal government, most states, and in some cases, local governments. Basic US federal income tax rates are listed below:

- Individual income tax rates are marginal, in that they increase as taxable income increases. Tax rates begin at 10 percent once $8,925 in taxable income is earned (for single and married filing separately taxpayers, married filed jointly amount begins at $17,850) and increase until they reach the highest rate of 39.6 percent (at approximately $400,001 in income for a single and married filing separately taxpayers, and $450,001 for married filing jointly taxpayers).

- Capital gains (gains from the sale of capital assets such as stocks and investment real estate) are taxed based on the holding period of the asset and the type of asset that is sold. In general, if the asset was held for less than one year, it is taxed at the same rate as income in the category above. If the asset was held for more than one year, it is taxed at a rate of 15 percent. Sales of collectibles are taxed at higher rates.
- US federal corporate tax rates are also marginal and generally begin at 15 percent and can be as high as 40 percent.
- Additional state income taxes (and city tax) may be imposed in certain states and cities; these can be as high as 14 percent and are assessed in addition to your federal income tax.

What happens if I don't comply with the tax laws?

Noncompliance penalties with the US tax laws are severe and can include criminal liability. While the scope of this presentation is not large enough to encompass all of the potential penalties for not meeting filing obligations, here are some common penalties that an LPR can face:

- Failure to file a US tax return—Penalty is 5 percent of the balance due plus and additional 5 percent per month, up to a maximum of 25 percent of the tax due.
- Failure to pay taxes when due—Penalty is .5 percent of the amount of the unpaid tax per month up to a maximum of 25 percent.
- Accuracy related penalties—If the amounts reported on an income tax return are later adjusted by the IRS and a tax increase results, an additional penalty may be assessed of 20 percent - 40 percent of the increase of the taxes due in some cases.
- Fraud penalties—If you fail to file a return or pay tax due and the IRS can demonstrate fraud, you can be liable to penalties that amount to 75 percent of the unpaid tax, and criminal prosecution.
- Taxpayers who are shareholders of corporations that are controlled by US persons (controlled foreign corporations) are required to file an annual disclosure statement. If such form is not filed in a timely manner, penalties can be assessed at $10,000 to $50,000 per form.
- Failure to file Statement of Specified Foreign Financial Assets—up to $10,000 for failure to disclose and an additional $10,000 for each thirty days of nonfiling after IRS notice for a failure to disclose; for a potential maximum penalty of $60,000; criminal penalties many also apply.

- Failure to disclose foreign bank and financial accounts can carry (among other penalties) the greater of $100,000 or 50 percent of the account balances, interest, and also criminal penalties, which may include arrest and prosecution (in the case of an LPR likely removal/deportation).

Potential criminal liability

Possible criminal charges related to tax returns include tax evasion (26 USC § 7201), filing a false return (26 USC § 7206(1)), and failure to file an income tax return (26 USC § 7203). Willfully failing to file an FBAR and willfully filing a false FBAR are both violations that are subject to criminal penalties under 31 USC § 5322.

A person convicted of tax evasion is subject to a prison term of up to five years and a fine of up to $250,000. Filing a false return subjects a person to a prison term of up to three years and a fine of up to $250,000. A person who fails to file a tax return is subject to a prison term of up to one year and a fine of up to $100,000. Failing to file an FBAR subjects a person to a prison term of up to ten years and criminal penalties of up to $500,000.

b. Business

Business taxes may be assessed against your enterprise at a federal, state, or local level. Due to the complexity of the regulatory environment this section will only discuss federal taxes from a very general perspective. Taxes are assessed and determined based on both business activity and the legal form of the enterprise.

Corporations

When most people discuss business taxation in the United States they are referring to corporate taxation. A corporation is an independent legal entity that is separate from the people who own it. Corporations are established under state law and are taxed on their income at both a state and federal level. Distributions from corporations can also be taxable in the form of dividends to the recipients, and this tax will be paid even on funds that were taxed at the corporate level, which gives rise to the complaint of double taxation of corporate profits.

Corporate tax rates on the federal level vary from 15 percent to 35 percent. These taxes are assessed against the net taxable income of the corporation.

State corporate tax rates can be an additional 4.63 percent (Colorado) to 12 percent (Iowa) on the taxable income of the corporation. It is important to note that not all states assess a corporate income tax.

Flow-through entities

A flow-through entity is a legal entity whose income or loss and other tax characteristics "flow through" to its owners. These entities are formed under state law and take the form of limited-liability companies, partnerships (limited partnerships and general partnerships), and small business (or subchapter S) corporations.

Because the entities are not taxed on their income at the entity level, the income or loss is reported on the owner's tax return. Therefore, this income is subject to the same rates as individuals, and taxes are levied at the individual owner's level.

Other business taxes may be assessed, depending on a specific type of business or licenses; therefore, it is advisable that you check with an attorney or accountant who is familiar with the tax rules and regulations in your location.

c. Estate Taxes

What is the estate tax?

Assuming that you are a US taxpayer, the estate tax is a tax on your right to transfer property at your death. It consists of an accounting of everything you own or have certain interests in at the date of death. The fair market value of these items is used, not necessarily what you paid for them or what their values were when you acquired them. The total of all of these items is your "gross estate." The includable property may consist of cash and securities, real estate, insurance, trusts, annuities, business interests, and other assets.

Once you have accounted for the gross estate, certain deductions (and in special circumstances, reductions to value) are allowed in arriving at your taxable estate. These deductions may include mortgages and other debts, estate administration expenses, property that passes to surviving spouses, and qualified charities. The value of some operating business interests or farms may be reduced for estates that qualify.

After the net amount is computed, the value of lifetime taxable gifts (beginning with gifts made in 1977) is added to this number, and the tax is computed. The tax is then reduced by the available unified credit.

Most relatively simple estates (cash, publicly traded securities, small amounts of other easily valued assets, and no special deductions or elections, or jointly held property) do not require the filing of an estate tax return. A filing is required for estates with combined gross assets and prior taxable gifts exceeding $1,500,000 in 2004–2005; $2,000,000 in 2006–2008; $3,500,000 for decedents dying in 2009; and $5,000,000 or more for decedent's dying in 2010 and 2011 (note: there are special rules for decedents dying in 2010); $5,120,000 in 2012, $5,250,000 in 2013, and $5,340,000 in 2014.

Beginning January 1, 2011, estates of decedents survived by a spouse may elect to pass any of the decedent's unused exemption to the surviving spouse. This election is made on a timely filed estate tax return for the decedent with a surviving spouse. Note that simplified valuation provisions apply for those estates without a filing requirement absent the portability election.

What is included in the estate?

The gross estate of the decedent consists of an accounting of everything you own or have certain interests in at the date of death. The fair market value of these items is used, not necessarily what you paid for them or what their values were when you acquired them. The total of all of these items is your gross estate. The includable property may consist of cash and securities, real estate, insurance, trusts, annuities, business interests and other assets. Keep in mind that the gross estate will likely include non-probate as well as probate property.

What is excluded from the estate?

Generally, the gross estate does not include property owned solely by the decedent's spouse or other individuals. Lifetime gifts that are complete (no powers or other control over the gifts are retained) are not included in the gross estate (but taxable gifts are used in the computation of the estate tax). Life estates given to the decedent by others, in which the decedent has no further control or power at the date of death, are not included.

What deductions are available to reduce the estate tax?

1. Marital deduction: One of the primary deductions for married decedents is the marital deduction. All property that is included in the gross estate and passes to the surviving spouse is eligible for the marital deduction. The property must pass outright. In some cases, certain life estates also qualify for the marital deduction.
2. Charitable deduction: If the decedent leaves property to a qualifying charity, it is deductible from the gross estate.
3. Mortgages and debt.
4. Administration expenses of the estate.
5. Losses during estate administration.

Estate tax rates

The estate tax begins at 18 percent and is as high as 40 percent. The following chart provides the current rates.

Lower Limit	Upper Limit	Initial Taxation	Further Taxation
0	$10,000	$0	18 percent of the amount
$10,000	$20,000	$1,800	20 percent of the excess
$20,000	$40,000	$3,800	22 percent of the excess
$40,000	$60,000	$8,200	24 percent of the excess
$60,000	$80,000	$13,000	26 percent of the excess
$80,000	$100,000	$18,200	28 percent of the excess
$100,000	$150,000	$23,800	30 percent of the excess
$150,000	$250,000	$38,800	32 percent of the excess
$250,000	$500,000	$70,800	34 percent of the excess
$500,000	$750,000	$155,800	37 percent of the excess
$750,000	$1,000,000	$248,300	39 percent of the excess
$1,000,000	and over	$345,800	40 percent of the excess

State estate taxes

In addition to federal estate taxes, several states also assess an estate tax. While these are the minority, this may impact the value of your estate and should be taken into consideration when deciding where to live or retire.

These states are currently: Delaware, Rhode Island, Washington, Connecticut, Hawaii, Maine, Maryland, Massachusetts, Minnesota, New Jersey, New York, North Carolina, Ohio, Oregon, Tennessee, Vermont, and the District of Columbia.

Estate taxes for nonresidents and non-US taxpayers

Deceased nonresidents who were not American citizens are subject to US estate taxation with respect to their US-situated assets.

US-situated assets include American real estate, tangible personal property, and securities of US companies. A nonresident's stock holdings in American companies are subject to estate taxation, even though the nonresident held the certificates abroad or registered the certificates in the name of a nominee.

Exceptions: Assets that are exempt from US estate tax include securities that generate portfolio interest, bank accounts not used in connection with a trade or business in the United States, and insurance proceeds.

Estate tax treaties between the United States and other countries often provide more favorable tax treatment to nonresidents by limiting the types of asset considered situated in the United States and subject to US estate taxation. Executors for nonresident estates should consult such treaties where applicable. Executors for nonresidents must file an estate tax return, if the fair market value at death of the decedent's US-situated assets exceeds $60,000. However, if the decedent made substantial lifetime gifts of US property, and used the applicable $13,000 "unified credit exemption" amount to eliminate or reduce any gift tax on the lifetime gifts, a US estate tax return may still be required, even if the value of the decedent's US-situated assets is less than $60,000 at the date of death (due to the decrease in the unified credit exemption for the lifetime gifts).

The Internal Revenue Service may collect any unpaid estate tax from any person receiving a distribution of the decedent's property under transferee liability provisions of the tax code.

d. Gift Taxes

Gift taxes in general

The gift tax is a tax on the transfer of property by one individual to another. The tax applies whether the donor intends the transfer to be a gift or not. The gift tax applies to the transfer by gift of any property. You make a gift if you give property (including money), or the use of or income from property, without expecting to receive something of at least equal value in return. If you sell something at less than its full value, or if you make an interest-free or reduced-interest loan, you may be making a gift.

Who pays the gift tax?

The donor is generally responsible for paying the gift tax. Under special arrangements the donee may agree to pay the tax instead. Please visit with your tax professional if you are considering this type of arrangement.

What is considered a gift?

Any transfer to an individual, either directly or indirectly, where full consideration (measured in money or money's worth) is not received in return.

What can be excluded from gifts?

The general rule is that any gift is a taxable gift. However, there are many exceptions to this rule. Generally, the following gifts are not taxable gifts:

- gifts that are not more than the annual exclusion for the calendar year
- tuition or medical expenses you pay for someone (the educational and medical exclusions)
- gifts to your spouse
- gifts to a political organization for its use

In addition to this, gifts to qualifying charities are deductible from the value of the gift(s) made.

How many annual exclusions are available?

The annual exclusion applies to gifts to each donee. In other words, if you give each of your children $11,000 in 2002–2005, $12,000 in 2006–2008, $13,000 in 2009–2012, and $14,000 on or after January 1, 2013, the annual exclusion applies to each gift.

What if my spouse and I want to give away property that we own together?

You are each entitled to the annual exclusion amount on the gift. Together, you can give $22,000 to each donee (2002–2005), $24,000 (2006–2008), $26,000 (2009–2012), and $28,000 on or after January 1, 2013.

e. Foreign asset reporting

The FBAR

If you have a financial interest in, or signature authority over, a foreign financial account that at any time during the year exceeded $10,000 (in aggregate), including a bank account, brokerage account, mutual fund, trust, or other type of foreign financial account, the Bank Secrecy Act requires you to report the account yearly to the Internal Revenue Service by filing electronically a Financial Crimes Enforcement Network (FinCEN) Form 114, *Report of Foreign Bank and Financial Accounts* (FBAR).

Overseas financial accounts are maintained by US persons for a variety of legitimate reasons, including convenience and access. The FBAR is required because foreign financial institutions may not be subject to the same reporting requirements as domestic financial institutions. The FBAR is also a tool used by the US government to identify persons who may be using foreign financial accounts to circumvent US law. Information contained in FBARs can be used to identify or trace funds used for illicit purposes or to identify unreported income maintained or generated abroad.

Who Must File the FBAR?

A US person must file an FBAR if that person has a financial interest in, or signature authority over, any financial account(s) outside of the United States, and the aggregate maximum value of the account(s) exceeds $10,000 *at any time* during the calendar year.

Who is a US person?

A "US person" means

- a citizen or resident of the United States,
- an entity created or organized in the United States or under the laws of the United States. The term "entity" includes but is not limited to, a corporation, partnership, and limited-liability company.
- a trust formed under the laws of the United States, or
- an estate formed under the laws of the United States.

Disregarded entities: Entities that are US persons and are disregarded for tax purposes may be required to file an FBAR. The federal tax treatment of an entity does not affect the entity's requirement to file an FBAR. FBARs are required under a Bank Secrecy Act provision of Title 31 and not under any provisions of the Internal Revenue Code.

US resident: A US resident is an alien residing in the United States. To determine if the filer is a resident of the United States, apply the residency tests in 26 USC § 7701(b). When applying the § 7701(b) residency tests, use the following definition of United States: United States includes the states, the District of Columbia, all US territories and possessions (e.g., American Samoa, the Commonwealth of the Northern Mariana Islands, the Commonwealth of Puerto Rico, Guam, and the US Virgin Islands), and the Indian lands as defined in the Indian Gaming Regulatory Act.

Financial account

"Financial account" includes the following types of accounts:

- bank accounts such as savings accounts, checking accounts, and time deposits
- securities accounts such as brokerage accounts and securities derivatives or other financial instruments accounts
- commodity futures or options accounts
- insurance policies with a cash value (such as a whole life insurance policy)
- mutual funds or similar pooled funds (i.e., a fund that is available to the general public with a regular net asset value determination and regular redemptions)
- any other accounts maintained in a foreign financial institution or with a person performing the services of a financial institution

Maximum account value—The maximum value of an account is a reasonable approximation of the greatest value of currency or nonmonetary assets in the account during the calendar year. Periodic account statements may be relied upon to determine the maximum value of the account, provided that the statements fairly reflect the maximum account value during the calendar year.

How to determine the maximum value of a foreign financial account— Determine the maximum account value in the currency of the account. After the maximum value of the account is determined, convert the maximum account value for each account into US dollars, using the exchange rate on the last day of the calendar year.

When converting between a foreign currency and US dollars, use the Treasury Reporting Rates of Exchange for the last day of the calendar year. If no Treasury Financial Management Service rate is available, use another verifiable exchange rate and provide the source of that rate. In valuing currency of a country that uses multiple exchange rates, use the rate that would apply if the currency in the account were converted into US dollars on the last day of the calendar year.

Financial interest—A US person has a financial interest in the following situations:

1. The US person is the owner of record or holder of legal title, regardless of whether the account is maintained for benefit of the US person or for the benefit of another person, including non-US persons.
2. The owner of record or holder of legal title is a person acting as an agent, nominee, attorney, or a person acting on behalf of the US person with respect to the account.
3. The owner of record or holder of legal title is a corporation in which a US person owns directly or indirectly: (i) more than 50 percent of the total value of shares of stock, or (ii) more than 50 percent of the voting power of all shares of stock.
4. The owner of record or holder of legal title is a partnership in which the US person owns directly or indirectly: (i) an interest in more than 50 percent of the partnership's profits (distributive share of partnership income taking into account any special allocation agreement), or (ii) an interest in more than 50 percent of the partnership capital.
5. The owner of record or holder of legal title is a trust of which the US person: (i) is the trust grantor and (ii) has an ownership interest in the trust for US federal tax purposes. See 26 USC §§ 671–679 to determine if a grantor has an ownership interest in a trust.

6. The owner of record or holder of legal title is a trust in which the US person has a greater than 50 percent present beneficial interest in the assets or income of the trust for the calendar year.
7. The owner of record or holder of legal title is any other entity in which the US person owns directly or indirectly more than 50 percent of the voting power, total value of equity interest or assets, or interest in profits.

Reporting jointly held accounts

If two persons jointly maintain a foreign financial account, or if several persons each own a partial interest in an account, then each US person has a financial interest in that account, and each person must report the entire value of the account on an FBAR.

Limited joint filing by spouses

The spouse of an individual who files an FBAR is not required to file a separate FBAR if the following conditions are met: (1) all the financial accounts that the nonfiling spouse is required to report are jointly owned with the filing spouse, (2) the filing spouse reports the jointly owned accounts on a timely filed FBAR electronically signed (PIN) in item 44, and (3) the filers have completed and signed Form 114a, Record of Authorization to Electronically File FBARs (maintained with the filers records). Otherwise, both spouses are required to file separate FBARs, and each spouse must report the entire value of the jointly owned accounts.

Filing exceptions

The following persons are excepted from the FBAR filing requirement:
olidated FBAR. A United States person that is an entity and is named in a consolidated FBAR filed by a greater than 50 percent owner is not required to file a separate FBAR.

- **IRA owners and beneficiaries.** An owner or beneficiary of an IRA is not required to report a foreign financial account held in the IRA.
- **Participants in and beneficiaries of tax-qualified retirement plans**. A participant in or beneficiary of a retirement plan described in Internal Revenue Code § 401(a), 403(a), or 403(b) is not required to report a foreign financial account held by or on behalf of the retirement plan.

Signature authority

Signature authority is the authority of an individual (alone or in conjunction with another individual) to control the disposition of assets held in a foreign financial account by direct communication (whether in writing or otherwise) to the bank or other financial institution that maintains the financial account.

Individuals who have signature authority over, but no financial interest in, a foreign financial account are not required to report the account in the following situations:

1. An officer or employee of a bank that is examined by the Office of the Comptroller of the Currency, the Board of Governors of the Federal Reserve System, the Federal Deposit Insurance Corporation, the Office of Thrift Supervision, or the National Credit Union Administration is not required to report signature authority over a foreign financial account owned or maintained by the bank.

2. An officer or employee of a financial institution that is registered with and examined by the Securities and Exchange Commission or Commodity Futures Trading Commission is not required to report signature authority over a foreign financial account owned or maintained by the financial institution.

3. An officer or employee of an authorized service provider is not required to report signature authority over a foreign financial account that is owned or maintained by an investment company that is registered with the Securities and Exchange Commission. Authorized service provider means an entity that is registered with and examined by the Securities and Exchange Commission and provides services to an investment company registered under the Investment Company Act of 1940.

4. An officer or employee of an entity that has a class of equity securities listed (or American depository receipts listed) on any US national securities exchange is not required to report signature authority over a foreign financial account of such entity.

5. An officer or employee of a US subsidiary is not required to report signature authority over a foreign financial account of the subsidiary if its US parent has a class of equity securities listed on any US national securities exchange and the subsidiary is included in a consolidated FBAR report of the US parent.

6. An officer or employee of an entity that has a class of equity securities registered (or American depository receipts in respect of equity securities registered) under section 12(g) of the Securities Exchange Act is not required to report signature authority over a foreign financial account of such entity.

Trust beneficiaries

A trust beneficiary with a direct or indirect financial interest in more than 50 percent of the trust assets or income is not required to report the trust's foreign financial accounts on an FBAR if the trust, trustee of the trust, or agent of the trust: (1) is a United States person and (2) files an FBAR disclosing the trust's foreign financial accounts.

Foreign financial accounts

The following types of foreign financial accounts are excepted from the FBAR filing requirement:

Certain accounts jointly owned by spouses—The spouse of an individual who files an FBAR is not required to file a separate FBAR if certain conditions are met as previously discussed; refer to the section about "reporting jointly held accounts."

Correspondent/nostro account—Correspondent or nostro accounts (maintained by banks and used solely for bank-to-bank settlements) are not required to be reported.

Governmental entity—A foreign financial account of any governmental entity is not required to be reported by any person.

International financial institution—A foreign financial account of any international financial institution (if the US government is a member) is not required to be reported by any person. Examples are the World Bank and the International Monetary Fund (IMF).

US military banking facility

A financial account maintained with a financial institution located on a US military installation is not required to be reported, even if that military installation is outside of the United States.

Record keeping

Generally, records of accounts required to be reported on the FBAR should be kept for five years from the due date of the report, which is June 30 of the year following the calendar year being reported. The records should contain the following:

- name maintained on each account
- number or other designation of the account
- name and address of the foreign bank or other person with whom the account is maintained

- type of account
- maximum value of each account during the reporting period

Retaining a copy of the filed FBAR can help to satisfy the record keeping requirements. However, an officer or employee who files an FBAR to report signature authority over an employer's foreign financial account is not required to personally retain records regarding these foreign financial accounts.

Penalties

Failure to file an FBAR when required to do so may result in civil penalties, criminal penalties, or both. When a US person learns that an FBAR should have been filed for a previous year, the filer should electronically file the delinquent FBAR report using the BSA E-Filing System website. The system allows the filer to enter the calendar year reported, including past years, on the online FinCEN Form 114. It also offers an option to "explain a late filing" or to select "other" to enter up to 750 characters within a text box where the filer can provide a further explanation of the late filing or indicate whether the filing is made in conjunction with an IRS compliance program. If the foreign financial account is properly reported on a late-filed FBAR, and the IRS determines that the FBAR violation was due to reasonable cause, no penalty will be imposed.

Due date

The FBAR is a calendar year report and must be received by the Department of Treasury on or before June 30 of the year following the calendar year being reported. The granting by the IRS of an extension to file federal income tax returns does not extend the due date for filing an FBAR. Filers cannot request an extension of the FBAR due date.

IRS Form 8938

Taxpayers with specified foreign financial assets that exceed certain thresholds must report those assets to the IRS on Form 8938, Statement of Specified Foreign Financial Assets, which is filed with an income tax return. The new Form 8938 filing requirement is in addition to the FBAR filing requirement.

f. Pre-immigration structuring

Prior to establishing your status as a US tax resident you may arrange your affairs to take advantages of legal structures or gifting that may have a material effect on your tax liabilities in the future. It is a good idea to meet with a competent US CPA or tax attorney, who has extensive international expertise and can help you with this planning and structuring process.

It is also a good idea to meet with a professional to fully understand the tax implications (federal income tax, state income tax, and estate tax) of your move to the United States.

g. Federal vs. state and local

You will be required to pay federal taxes, and you also may be subject to taxation at both a state and local level. If you are unsure of your reporting responsibilities, you should contact a tax preparer in your location who understands the reporting requirements specific to that jurisdiction.

State and local income taxes can have a large effect on your income. Some states do not assess a tax, some assess taxes only on dividends and interest, and some can assess a combined tax up to 12 percent or more of your income. It is important to understand the tax environment of the place that you plan to move to.

h. Personal property taxes

Personal property taxes are only assessed at a state level. These taxes may be levied against different types of property. In some states, this applies only to property that you own that produces income; in other states, this may include cars, boats, or other property that you merely own. Some states may assess taxes against vehicles that are leased from their states, so if you lease a vehicle, you may receive a personal property tax bill from a location that you may have never even been to.

Before you pay any personal property tax bill, it is a good idea to check with an experienced tax preparer to ensure that you are paying the correct amount.

i. Sales taxes

Sales taxes are taxes that are imposed by state and local governments on the sale or lease of goods or services. If you are a consumer, these taxes will be collected at the time of transaction and remitted to the property authority. Currently forty-five states impose a general sales tax. Sales taxes are rarely included in the cost of the item that is quoted or on the price, so be aware that you will need to add this amount when determining the final cost. Sales taxes can range from 0 percent to a combined rate of 12 percent (as in the case of Arkansas).

If you are the seller or provider you will need to collect and remit these taxes. This can be a complex and confusing process, and if you are just starting out in a new business, it is advisable to find a qualified tax practitioner who can help you determine your collection and payment responsibilities. Penalties for not adhering to the sales tax collection and payment requirements can be severe.

Chapter 7:

HEALTH CARE

Health care in the United States is considered excellent by international standards. However, health care can be very expensive if you do not have insurance. Having health insurance allows you to get the treatment that you need without incurring huge medical bills. Recent legislation now requires that all American taxpayers obtain and maintain health insurance or pay a penalty.

The health-care system in the United States is large and is provided by many different organizations and both public and private sector resources. In the United States, 62 percent of the hospitals are nonprofit, 20 percent are government owned, and 18 percent are for profit. According to the World Health Organization, the United States spent more on health care per capita ($8,068) than any other nation in 2011, amounting to almost 17.2 percent of its gross domestic product.

Under recent legislation, the Affordable Care Act, all Americans can get health insurance regardless of income and health history. Aside from private insurance, there are two primary government programs for proving health benefits.

a. The US health-care system

Taking care of your health

People in the United States pay for their own medical care. Medical care is expensive, so many people buy health insurance. You should get health insurance for yourself and your family as soon as possible.

Employers may offer health insurance as a benefit to their employees. Some employers pay all of your monthly health insurance fee, and some pay only part of the fee. This monthly fee is called a premium. You may need to pay part of the premium. Usually, employers will deduct the employee's part of the premium from his or her paycheck.

Doctors send their bills to your health insurance company. The health insurance company will pay for some or all of your medical services. Often you must pay a portion of your medical bills. This is sometimes called a "copayment."

If you do not have health insurance, you may be able to get federal or state health-care assistance. In general, most states provide some type of assistance to children and pregnant women. Check with the public health department of your state or town. If you need urgent medical care, you can go to the emergency room of the nearest hospital. Most hospitals are required by federal law to treat patients with a medical emergency, even if the person cannot pay.

Finding a clinic or other low-cost health care

Clinics are medical offices that provide free or low-cost services. Most communities have at least one clinic. Community organizations that work with immigrants may know of a low-cost or free clinic in your area.

The US Department of Health and Human Services also provides basic health care to immigrants. They have a website that lists clinics and other health-care choices. To find a clinic or doctor near you, visit www.ask.hrsa.gov/pc/. Type in your state or zip code to get the information. You can also look in the yellow pages under "Social Services."

b. Coverage

Federal and state health programs

Medicaid is a joint federal/state program for low-income people. Each state has its own Medicaid guidelines. Medicaid pays for medical services, such as visits to the doctor and hospitalization. Permanent residents who entered the United States before August 22, 1996, may be able to get Medicaid if they meet certain conditions. Permanent residents who entered the United States on or after August 22, 1996, may be able to get Medicaid if they have lived in the United States for five years or longer and meet certain conditions.

Medicare is a health insurance program for people sixty-five years of age or older, or who have specific disabilities. Medicare pays for services if you are sick or injured, but does not pay for routine care (such as checkups with your doctor), dental care, or eye care.

Medicare has several parts, including Part A, Part B, and prescription drug coverage. Part A is free and pays for hospital care and nursing homes certified by Medicare. Part B pays for visits to the doctor, ambulances, tests, and outpatient hospital care. For Part B, you pay a monthly fee. Prescription drug coverage helps pay for medications doctors prescribe for treatment. Enrolling in a Medicare prescription drug plan is voluntary, and you pay an additional monthly fee for this coverage.

Permanent residents can get Medicare Part A, Part B, and prescription drug coverage if they meet certain conditions. Those who are sixty-five and older are automatically in Medicare when they start getting Social Security retirement benefits. If you are not sixty-five but are eligible for other reasons, call the Social Security office near you for information about enrolling. Generally, you must have worked in the United States for ten years (or forty quarters) over the course of your life to get these Medicare benefits. For more information, download the publication *Medicare & You* from the Medicare website at www.medicare.gov/Pubs/pdf/10050.pdf

More information about Medicaid and Medicare

Contact the Social Security Administration at (800) 772-1213 or the Centers for Medicare and Medicaid Service website at www.cms.hhs.gov. State Children's Health Insurance Program (SCHIP): Your children may be able to get free or low-cost health care if you meet certain conditions. Every state has a health insurance program for infants, children, and teenagers. The insurance pays for doctor visits, prescription medicines, hospital care, and other health-care services. In most states, children eighteen and younger without health insurance whose families meet certain income limits are eligible. Children can get free or low-cost health care without affecting their parents' immigration status.

c. Maternity

General facts on women and job-based health insurance

Approximately 80 percent of women age eighteen to sixty-four had health insurance in 2011. The remaining 20 percent—which translates into nineteen million women—had no health benefit coverage. Eighteen percent of women obtained insurance from public programs, including Medicaid, Medicare, and CHAMPUS. Sixty-seven percent had private insurance. Private insurance was obtained mainly through employment-based plans. Sixty percent of all women had such coverage, either in their own names or as dependents, 45 percent through private-sector jobs and 15 percent through government jobs. Women utilize more health care than men, in part because of their need for reproductive services. Females of all ages accounted for 57 percent of all expenses incurred at doctors' offices in 2011. Women make approximately 80 percent of health care decisions for their families and are more likely to be the caregivers when a family member falls ill.

d. Public benefits and assistance

Other federal benefits programs—You or members of your family may be eligible for other federal benefits, depending on your immigration status, length of time in the United States, and income.

The food stamp program—Some low-income immigrants and immigrant children may be eligible for food stamp assistance, depending on their immigration status, length of time in the United States, and income. Food stamps allow you to obtain some foods free at grocery stores. Some states may have their own state-funded food stamp programs with different rules for immigrant eligibility, and these may vary from state to state. For information on federal food stamp eligibility from the US Food and Nutrition Service in thirty-six different languages, visit www.fns.usda.gov/fsp/outreach/translations.htm.

Services for survivors of domestic violence—Immigrants and their children who are survivors of domestic violence may be eligible for federal benefits and services, such as battered women's shelters or food stamps. For more information on these services from the US Department of Health and Human Services, visit www.hhs.gov/ocr/immigration/bifsltr.html.

Temporary Assistance for Needy Families (TANF)—Temporary Assistance for Needy Families is a federal program that gives money to states to provide assistance and work opportunities for low-income families. Immigrants may be eligible, depending on their immigration status, length of time in the United States, and income. Programs differ by state, and some states have their own state-funded assistance programs. For links and information on TANF, visit www.acf.dhhs.gov/programs/ofa/.

Chapter 8:

INSURANCE

a. Auto Insurance

Auto insurance protects you from financial losses resulting from an accident, theft, or vandalism associated with your vehicle. You contract with an insurance company for this coverage and pay them either a monthly, quarterly, or annual premium for the coverage. The cost of coverage depends on the value of the car, your US driving history, location of the vehicle, annual miles driven, and the type of coverage that you select (among other things).

Auto insurance can also provide you with medical coverage, which pays for the treatment and rehabilitation of injuries, coverage for funeral costs, or even lost wages as the result of an accident. Liability coverage will provide coverage to others in the event that you are at fault in an accident that results in damage to another person's property or injury. There are six primary types of auto insurance coverage:

- property damage liability
- bodily injury liability
- comprehensive insurance
- collision
- medical payments or personal injury protection
- uninsured or underinsured motorist coverage

Most states require that you carry a minimum amount of liability insurance in order to legally operate a vehicle, and if you do not have insurance you can be fined or, in some cases, arrested.

b. Home

See previous section on homeowners insurance (chapter 2).

c. Health

Health insurance is a program that helps you pay for medical expenses. Health insurance generally falls into one of three categories: group policies through your employer, Medicare and Medicaid, and individual plans.

Group policies

Many consumers have health-care coverage from their employer. Others have medical care paid through a government program such as Medicare, Medicaid, or the Veterans Administration. If you have lost your group coverage from an employer as the result of unemployment, death, divorce, or loss of "dependent child" status, you may be able to continue your coverage temporarily under the Consolidated Omnibus Budget Reconciliation Act (COBRA). You, not the employer, pay for this coverage. When one of these events occurs, you must be given at least sixty days to decide whether you wish to purchase the coverage.

Some states offer an insurance pool to residents who are unable to obtain coverage because of a health condition. To find out if a pool is available in your state, check with your state department of insurance.

Medicare and Medicaid

There are also health insurance programs for people who are seniors, disabled, or have low incomes.

- Medicaid provides health insurance for people with low incomes, children, and pregnant women. Eligibility is determined by your state.
- Medicare provides health insurance for people who are sixty-five years or older, some younger people with disabilities, and those with kidney failure.

Most states also offer free or low-cost coverage for children who do not have health insurance. Visit www.insurekidsnow.gov or call (877) KIDS-NOW (543-7669) for more information.

Individual health-care plans

When purchasing health insurance, your choices will typically fall into one of three categories:

- **Traditional fee-for-service health insurance plans** are usually the most expensive choice. But they offer you the most flexibility when choosing health-care providers.
- **Health maintenance organizations (HMOs)** offer lower copayments and cover the costs of more preventative care, but your choice of healthcare providers is limited. The National Committee for Quality Assurance evaluates and accredits HMOs. You can find out whether one is accredited in your state by calling (888) 275-7585. You can also get this information as well as report cards on HMOs.
- **Preferred provider organizations (PPOs)** offer lower copayments like HMOs but give you more flexibility when selecting a provider. A PPO gives you a list of providers you can choose from.

WARNING: If you go outside the HMO or PPO network of providers, you may have to pay a portion or all of the costs. When choosing among different health-care plans, you'll need to read the fine print and ask lots of questions, such as

- Do I have the right to go to any doctor, hospital, clinic, or pharmacy I choose?
- Are specialists such as eye doctors and dentists covered?
- Does the plan cover special conditions or treatments such as pregnancy, psychiatric care, and physical therapy?
- Does the plan cover home care or nursing home care?
- Will the plan cover all medications my physician might prescribe?
- What are the deductibles? Are there any copayments?
- What is the most I will have to pay out of my own pocket to cover expenses?

If there is a dispute about a bill or service, how is it handled? In some plans, you may be required to have a third-party decide how to settle the problem.

d. Umbrella

Umbrella insurance is a special type of liability insurance that insures against losses that are in excess of your other policies or that may not be specifically covered by your other policies. Examples of what umbrella insurance might cover may be liabilities in excess of your homeowners or other insurance policies for claims of injury or damage that are covered under the policy. Umbrella insurance can also cover claims for things that are not covered by your other policies such as libel, slander, false arrest, coverage for vacation, or rental properties.

e. Life

Life insurance is a contract with an insurance company; the insurance company will provide a lump-sum payment to the designated beneficiaries of the policy in the event of the death of the person who is insured. A premium is paid in exchange for this type of insurance. Costs of the premiums are usually determined by the insured's health, age, family medical history, lifestyle (things such as tobacco use increase the cost), and the type and duration of policy. Life insurance benefits are generally income tax-free when received.

Your need for life insurance will change with changes in your life. For example, the arrival of children usually triggers a sharp increase in the amount you need. As children grow older and leave the nest, you will probably need less protection.

Term life insurance policies are the least costly. They pay death benefits but have no cash value if you decide to stop making payments. As the word "term" suggests, these policies are in effect for a specific period of time—one year or until you reach a certain age are common. You can compare life insurance policies online.

Whole life, universal life, and other cash value policies combine a long-term savings and investment product with life insurance. Canceling these policies after only a few years can more than double your life insurance costs.

f. Disability

Disability can be more disastrous financially than death. If you are disabled, you lose your earning power, but you still have living expenses and often huge expenses for medical care. Disability insurance helps you replace lost income.

Many employers offer some type of disability insurance coverage for employees, or you can get an individual disability insurance policy. There are two types of disability policies: short-term disability (STD) and long-term disability (LTD). Short-term disability policies have a maximum benefit of two years, while long-term disability policies have benefits that can last the rest of your life.

Chapter 9:

RETIREMENT

a. The Retirement System in the US

The retirement system in the United States is a combination of federal benefits (such as Social Security), private savings, tax deferred savings accounts, and employer sponsored retirement benefits—such as defined contribution plans, or defined benefit plans such as pensions.

The Social Security system only provides less than half of the income that most Americans earned while working; therefore, the US system is highly subsidized by private savings.

b. Social Security

Social Security reaches almost every family and at some point will touch the lives of nearly all Americans.

Social Security helps not only older Americans, but also workers who become disabled and families in which a spouse or parent dies. Today, about 165 million people work and pay Social Security taxes and about 58 million people receive monthly Social Security benefits.

Most of social security beneficiaries are retirees and their families—about 41 million people.

But Social Security was never meant to be the only source of income for people when they retire. Social Security replaces about 40 percent of an average wage earner's income after retiring, and most financial advisers say retirees will need 70 percent or more of preretirement earnings to live comfortably. To have a comfortable retirement, Americans need much more than just Social Security. They also need private pensions, savings, and investments.

The current Social Security system works like this: when you work, you pay taxes into Social Security. The tax money is used to pay benefits to

- people who already have retired;
- people who are disabled;
- survivors of workers who have died; and
- dependents of beneficiaries.

The money you pay in taxes is not held in a personal account for you to use when you get benefits. Your taxes are being used right now to pay people who now are getting benefits. Any unused money goes to the Social Security trust funds, not a personal account with your name on it.

Social Security is more than retirement

Many people think of Social Security as just a retirement program. Although it is true that most of the people receiving Social Security receive retirement benefits, many others get Social Security because they are

- disabled; or
- a spouse or child of someone who gets Social Security; or
- a spouse or child of a worker who died; or
- a dependent parent of a worker who died.

Depending on your circumstances, you may be eligible for Social Security at any age. In fact, Social Security pays more benefits to children than any other government program.

Your Social Security taxes

The Social Security taxes you and other workers pay into the system are used to pay for Social Security benefits.

You pay Social Security taxes on your earnings up to a certain amount. In 2014, that amount is $117,000.

Medicare taxes

You pay Medicare taxes on all of your wages or net earnings from self-employment. These taxes are used for Medicare coverage.

If you work for someone else	Social Security tax	Medicare tax
You pay	6.2 percent	1.45 percent
Your employer Pays	6.2 percent	1.45 percent
If you are self-employed		
You pay	12.4 percent	2.9 percent

Additional Medicare tax

Workers pay an additional 0.9 percent Medicare tax on income exceeding certain thresholds. The following chart shows the threshold amounts based on tax filing status:

Filing Status	Threshold Amount
Married filing jointly	$250,000
Married filing separately	$125,000
Single	$200,000
Head of Household (with Qualifying person)	$200,000
Qualifying widow(er) with dependent child	$200,000

Where your Social Security tax dollars go

When you work, 85 cents of every Social Security tax dollar you pay goes to a trust fund that pays monthly benefits to current retirees and their families and to surviving spouses and children of workers who have died. The other 15 cents goes to a trust fund that pays benefits to people with disabilities and their families.

From these trust funds, Social Security also pays the costs of managing the Social Security programs. The Social Security Administration is one of the most efficient agencies in the federal government, and we are working to make it better every day. Of each Social Security tax dollar you pay, we spend less than one penny to manage the program. The entire amount of taxes you pay for Medicare goes to a trust fund that pays for some of the costs of hospital and related care of all Medicare beneficiaries. Medicare is managed by the Centers for Medicare and Medicaid Services, not Social Security.

Benefits and "full retirement age"

Social Security benefits replace a percentage of your earnings when you retire, become disabled, or die. Your benefit payment is based on how much you earned during your working career. Higher lifetime earnings result in higher benefits. If there were some years when you did not work or had low earnings, your benefit amount may be lower than if you worked steadily.

Retirement benefits

Choosing when to retire is one of the most important decisions you will make in your lifetime. If you choose to retire when you reach your full retirement age, you will receive your full benefit amount. But if you retire before reaching full retirement age, you will receive reduced benefits. The following chart lists the full retirement age by year of birth.

If you were born from 1943 to 1960, the age at which full retirement benefits are payable increases gradually to age 67. If you were born in 1947 or earlier, you already are eligible for your full Social Security benefit. The following chart will guide you in determining your full retirement age.

Delayed retirement

If you choose to delay receiving benefits beyond your full retirement age, your benefit will be increased by a certain percentage, depending on the year you were born. The increase will be added in automatically each month from the time you reach full retirement age until you start taking benefits or reach age seventy, whichever comes first. The percentage of the increase is based on when you were born. For more information on delayed retirement credits, go to www. socialsecurity.gov/retire2/delayret.htm.

Early retirement

You may start receiving benefits as early as age sixty-two. However, if you start your benefits early, your benefits are reduced. Your benefit is reduced about one-half of 1 percent for each month you start your Social Security before your full retirement age. For example, if your full retirement age is 66 and you sign up for Social Security when you are sixty-two, you would only get 75 percent of your full benefit.

NOTE: The reduction will be greater in future years as the full retirement age increases.

If you work and get benefits

You can continue to work and still receive retirement benefits. Your earnings in (or after) the month you reach full retirement age will not reduce your Social Security benefits. In fact, working beyond full retirement age can increase your benefits. However, your benefits will be reduced if your earnings exceed certain limits for the months before you reach your full retirement age.

If you work but start receiving benefits before full retirement age, $1 in benefits will be deducted for each $2 in earnings you have above the annual limit. In 2014, the limit is $15,480.

In the year you reach your full retirement age, your benefits will be reduced $1 for every $3 you earn over a different annual limit ($41,400 in 2014) until the month you reach full retirement age.

Once you reach full retirement age, you can keep working, and your Social Security benefit will not be reduced, no matter how much you earn.

For more information about how work affects your benefits, ask for *How Work Affects Your Benefits* (Publication No. 05-10069).

NOTE: People who work and receive disability or Supplemental Security Income payments have different earnings rules. They immediately must report all of their earnings to Social Security no matter how much they earn.

Retirement benefits for widows and widowers

If you are receiving widow's or widower's benefits, you can switch to your own retirement benefits as early as age sixty-two, assuming your retirement benefit is more than the amount you receive on your deceased spouse's earnings. In many cases, you can begin receiving one benefit at a reduced rate and then switch to the other benefit at the full rate when you reach full retirement age. The rules are complicated and vary, depending on your situation, so talk to a Social Security representative about the options available to you.

For more information about retirement benefits, ask for *Retirement Benefits* (Publication No. 05-10035).

Disability benefits

If you cannot work because of a physical or mental condition that is expected to last at least one year or result in death, you may be eligible for Social Security disability benefits.

Our disability rules are different from those of private plans or other government agencies. The fact that you qualify for disability from another agency or program does not mean you will be eligible for disability benefits from us. And having a statement from your doctor indicating you are disabled does not mean you will automatically be eligible for Social Security disability benefits. For more information about Social Security disability benefits, ask for *Disability Benefits* (Publication No. 05-10029). You can apply for Social Security disability benefits on our website at www.socialsecurity.gov/applyfordisability.

People with disabilities, including children, who have little income and few resources, also may be eligible for disability payments through the Supplemental Security Income (SSI) program. For more information about SSI, ask for *Supplemental Security Income (SSI)* (Publication No. 05-11000).

If you become disabled, you should file for disability benefits as soon as possible, because it usually takes several months to process a disability claim. They may be able to process your claim more quickly if you have the following when you apply:

- medical records and treatment dates from your doctors, therapists, hospitals, clinics and caseworkers
- your laboratory and other test results
- the names, addresses, phone, and fax numbers of your doctors, clinics, and hospitals
- the names of all medications you are taking, and
- the names of your employers and job duties for the last fifteen years

Your benefits may be taxable

Some people who get Social Security will have to pay taxes on their benefits. About 40 percent of our current beneficiaries pay taxes on their benefits.

You will have to pay taxes on your benefits if you file a federal tax return as an individual, and your total income is more than $25,000. If you file a joint return, you will have to pay taxes if you and your spouse have a total income that is more than $32,000. For more information, call the Internal Revenue Service's toll-free number, (800) 829-3676.

Benefits for your family

When you start receiving Social Security retirement or disability benefits, other family members also may be eligible for payments. For example, benefits can be paid to your husband or wife if

- he or she is age sixty-two or older, or
- at any age if he or she is caring for your child (the child must be younger than sixteen, or disabled and entitled to Social Security benefits on your record).

Benefits also can be paid to your unmarried children if they are

- younger than eighteen;
- between eighteen and nineteen years old, but in elementary or secondary school as full-time students; or
- age eighteen or older and severely disabled (the disability must have started before age twenty-two).

If you become the parent of a child (including an adopted child) after you begin receiving benefits, let us know about the child, so we can decide if the child is eligible for benefits.

How much can family members get?

Each family member may be eligible for a monthly benefit that is up to half of your retirement or disability benefit amount. However, there is a limit to the total amount of money that can be paid to you and your family. The limit varies, but is generally equal to about 150–180 percent of your retirement or disability benefit.

Benefits for ex-wives

If you are divorced, your ex-spouse may qualify for benefits on your earnings. In some situations, he or she may get benefits even if you are not receiving them. To qualify, a divorced spouse must

- have been married to you for at least ten years;
- have been divorced at least two years;
- be at least sixty-two years old;
- be unmarried; and
- not be eligible for an equal or higher benefit based on his or her own work or someone else's work.

Survivors benefits

When you die, your family may be eligible for benefits based on your work. Family members who can collect benefits include a widow or widower who is

- sixty or older; or
- fifty or older and disabled; or
- any age, if he or she is caring for your child who is younger than sixteen or disabled and entitled to Social Security benefits on your record.

Your children can receive benefits, too, if they are unmarried and

- younger than eighteen years old; or
- between eighteen and nineteen years old, but in an elementary or secondary school as full-time students; or
- age eighteen or older and severely disabled (the disability must have started before age twenty-two).

Additionally, your parents can receive benefits on your earnings if they were dependent on you for at least half of their support.

Payment after death

If you have enough credits, a one-time payment of $255 also may be made after your death. This benefit may be paid to your spouse or minor children if they meet certain requirements.

If you are divorced, your ex-spouse may be eligible for survivors benefits based on your earnings when you die. He or she must

- be at least age sixty years old (or fifty if disabled) and have been married to you for at least ten years; or
- be any age if he or she is caring for a child who is eligible for benefits based on your earnings; and

- not be eligible for an equal or higher benefit based on his or her own work; and
- not be currently married, unless the remarriage occurred after age sixty or after age fifty if disabled.

Benefits paid to an ex-spouse will not affect the benefit rates for other survivors receiving benefits on your earnings record.

NOTE: If you are deceased and your ex-spouse remarries after age sixty, he or she may be eligible for Social Security benefits based both on your work and the new spouse's work, whichever is higher.

How much will your survivors get?

Your survivors receive a percentage of your basic Social Security benefit—usually in a range of 75–100 percent each. However, there is a limit to the amount of money that can be paid each month to a family. The limit varies, but is generally equal to about 150–180 percent of your benefit rate.

Some Social Security facts
2014 Social Security taxes

- You pay 6.2 percent and your employer pays 6.2 percent.
- If you are self-employed, you pay 12.4 percent.
- You do not pay Social Security taxes on any earnings above $117,000.

2014 Medicare taxes

- You and your employer each pay 1.45 percent.
- If you are self-employed, you pay 2.9 percent.
- Medicare taxes are paid on all of your earnings; there is no limit.
- There are additional Medicare taxes for higher-income workers.

Work credits in 2014

- For each $1,200 you earn, you receive one Social Security "credit," up to four per year.
- Most people need forty credits to be eligible for retirement benefits.
- Younger people need fewer credits to qualify for disability benefits or for their family members to be eligible for survivors benefits.
- Average 2014 monthly Social Security benefits
    - Retired worker: $1,294

- o   Retired couple: $2,111
- o   Disabled worker: $1,148
- o   Disabled worker with a spouse and child: $1,943
- o   Widow or widower: $1,243
- o   Young widow or widower with two children: $2,622

2014 monthly SSI payment rates
(does not include state supplement, if any)

- $721 for an individual
- $1,082 for a couple

c. Retirement Plans

There are many types of retirement plans in the United States, and most have significant tax benefits associated with them. Almost all require that you contribute to them, some are solely funded by your employer (or yourself if you are the business owner). Some are funded entirely by you. Most offer the deferral (and in the case of the Roth IRA, the permanent nonrecognition of income or taxes) of income and taxes until you withdraw the funds, and they may provide for a deduction against your taxable income for contributions that you make.

There are two primary types of retirement plans, defined benefit plans and defined contributions plans.

Defined benefit plan

A defined benefit plan, funded by the employer, promises you a specific monthly benefit at retirement. The plan may state this promised benefit as an exact dollar amount, such as $100 per month at retirement. Or, more often, it may calculate your benefit through a formula that includes factors such as your salary, your age, and the number of years you worked at the company. For example, your pension benefit might be equal to 1 percent of your average salary for the last five years of employment times your total years of service.

Defined contribution plan

A defined contribution plan, on the other hand, does not promise you a specific benefit amount at retirement. Instead, you and/or your employer contribute money to your individual account in the plan. In many cases, you are responsible for choosing how these contributions are invested, and deciding how much to contribute from your paycheck through pretax deductions. Your employer may add to your account, in some cases by matching a certain percentage of your contributions. The value of your account depends on how much is contributed and how well the investments perform. At retirement, you receive the balance in your account, reflecting the contributions, investment gains or losses, and any fees charged against your account. The 401(k) plan is a popular type of defined contribution plan. There are four types of 401(k) plans: traditional 401(k), safe harbor 401(k), SIMPLE 401(k), and automatic enrollment 401(k) plans. The SIMPLE IRA plan, SEP, employee stock ownership plan (ESOP), and profit sharing plan are other examples of defined contribution plans.

d. Estate planning and trusts

People at all economic levels benefit from an estate plan. Upon death, an estate plan legally protects and distributes property based on your wishes and the needs of your family and survivors with as little tax as possible.

A will is the most practical first step in estate planning; it makes clear how you want your property to be distributed after you die.

Writing a will can be as simple as typing out how you want your assets to be transferred to loved ones or charitable organizations after your death. If you don't have a will when you die, your estate will be handled in probate, and your property could be distributed differently than what you would like.

The authors recommend that you get legal advice when writing and/or considering a will, particularly when it comes to understanding all the rules of the estate disposition process in your state. Some states, for instance, have community-property laws that entitle your surviving spouse to keep half of your wealth after you die no matter what percentage you leave him or her. Fees for the execution of a will vary according to its complexity.

One of the most common secondary elements of any estate plan is the trust.

e. Trusts

It is a common misconception that trusts, or trust funds as they are commonly called, are only useful for wealthy people. When set up properly, trusts can be appropriate for people with minor children or those who want to avoid having their estate go through probate upon death. These are basic facts about trusts—but be sure to consult a licensed attorney experienced with estate planning and trust matters before making any final decisions about whether one is right for you.

Chapter 10:

DIRECTORY OF SERVICE PROVIDERS AND RESOURCES

a. Attorneys

Overview

Legal Assistance: If you need help with an immigration issue, you can use the services of a licensed and competent immigration lawyer. You can check with your local bar association for help finding a qualified lawyer. Some states certify specialists in immigration law. These attorneys have passed tests to prove they have special knowledge about immigration law. The following are states that currently list certified specialists on their state bar websites: California, Florida, North Carolina, and Texas. Please note, however, that you are responsible for determining whether to hire a particular attorney. DHS does not endorse or recommend any particular attorney. If you need legal help on an immigration issue but you do not have enough money to hire a lawyer, there are some low-cost or free assistance options. You can ask for help from:

A recognized organization—The Board of Immigration Appeals (BIA) recognizes these organizations. For an organization to be "recognized," it must have enough knowledge and experience to provide services to immigrants and can charge or accept only very small fees for those services. For a list of these BIA-recognized organizations, see www.justice.gov/eoir/ra.htm.

An accredited representative—These people are connected to BIA "recognized organizations." These representatives can charge or accept only very small fees for their services. For a list of these BIA-accredited representatives, see www.justice.gov/eoir/ra.htm.

A qualified representative—These are people who will provide free services. These representatives must know about immigration law and the rules of practice in court. Examples of qualified representatives include law school students and graduates and people with good moral character who have a personal or professional affiliation with you (relative, neighbor, clergy, coworker, or friend).

Free legal service providers—The Office of the Chief Immigration Judge has a list of recognized free legal service providers for people who are in immigration proceedings (see www.usdoj.gov/eoir/probono/states.htm). This is a list of attorneys and organizations that may be willing to represent immigrants in proceedings before the immigration courts. The attorneys and organizations on this list have agreed to help immigrants *pro bono* (free of charge) only in immigration proceedings, so some of them may not be able to help you with noncourt-related matters (that is, visa petitions, naturalization, etc.).

Pro bono **program**—Local lists of recognized *pro bono* (free of charge) organizations and their representatives are usually available at each local USCIS office.

Contacts

American Immigration Lawyers Association
1331 G Street NW, Suite 300
Washington, DC 20005-3142
Phone: (202) 507-7600Fax: (202) 783-7853
www.aila.org

American Association for Justice
777 6th Street NW, Suite 200
Washington, DC 20001
Phone:(800) 424-2725 or (202) 965-3500
www.justice.org

American Bar Association
(ABA) Service Hotline:(800) 285-2221,(312) 988-5000
Monday–Friday9:00 a.m.–6:00 p.m. ET

Chicago Headquarters:
321 North Clark Street
Chicago, IL 60654
Phone:(312) 988-5000

Washington, DC Office:1050 Connecticut Ave. NW,Suite 400
Washington, DC 20036
Phone: (202) 662-1000
www.americanbar.org

Beware of immigration consultant fraud!

Many immigration practitioners are well qualified and honest and can provide good services to immigrants. However, there are some people who take advantage of immigrants.

Before you decide to get help with immigration matters, and before you pay any money, you should do some research so you can make the right decision about what kind of legal help you need. Protect yourself from becoming a victim of immigration fraud.

b. Accountants

American Institute of CPAs

Member Service Center: e-mail: service@aicpa.org
Phone: (888) 777-7077, Fax: (800) 362-5066
www.aicpa.org

Durham, NC:
220 Leigh Farm Road
Durham, NC 27707-8110
Phone: (919) 402-4500, Fax: (919) 402-4505

Ewing, NJ:
Princeton South Corporate Center 100 Princeton South, Suite 200
Ewing, NJ 08628
Phone: (609) 671-2902, Fax: (609) 671-2922

New York, NY:
1211 Avenue of the Americas

New York, NY 10036-8775
Phone: (212) 596-6200, Fax: (212) 596-6213

Washington, DC:
1455 Pennsylvania Ave. NW
Washington, DC 20004-1081
Phone: (202) 737-6600, Fax: (202) 638-4512

c. Realtors

Association of Realtors Headquarters
430 North Michigan Avenue
Chicago, IL 60611-4087

Washington, DC:
500 New Jersey Avenue NW
Washington, DC 20001-20201
Phone:(800) 874-6500
www.realtor.org

d. Insurance Agents

National Association of Professional Insurance Agents
400 North Washington Street
Alexandria, VA 22314
Phone: (703) 836-9340,Fax: (703) 836-1279
web@pianet.org.
www.pianet.com/contact

e. Medical Professionals

American Medical Association
Suite 39300
AMA Plaza
330 North Wabash Ave.
Chicago, IL 60611-5885

AMA Member Relations: (800) 262-3211
www.ama-assn.org/ama/home.page?

f. Government Sites

Federal departments and agencies—If you are not sure which department to call about a question, start by calling (800) FED-INFO (or (800) 333-4636) to ask where to call. People who have difficulty hearing can call (800) 326-2996. You can also visit www.USA.gov for general information about federal departments and agencies.

Department of Education (ED)
400 Maryland Avenue SW
Washington, DC 20202
Phone:(800) 872-5327, for hearing impaired: (800) 437-0833
www.ed.gov

Equal Employment Opportunity Commission (EEOC)
1801 L Street NW
Washington, DC 20507
Phone: (800) 669-4000, for hearing impaired: (800) 669-6820
www.eeoc.gov

Department of Health and Human Services (HHS)
200 Independence Avenue SW
Washington, DC 20201
Phone: (877) 696-6775
www.hhs.gov

Department of Homeland Security (DHS)
Washington, DC 20528
www.dhs.gov

US Citizenship and Immigration Services (USCIS)
Phone: (800) 375-5283, for hearing impaired: (800) 767-1833
www.uscis.gov

US Customs and Border Protection (CBP)
Phone: (202) 354-1000
www.cbp.gov

US Immigration and Customs Enforcement (ICE)
www.ice.gov

Department of Housing and Urban Development (HUD)
451 Seventh Street SW
Washington, DC 20410
Phone: (202) 708-1112, for hearing impaired: (202) 708-1455
www.hud.gov

Department of Justice (DOJ)
US Department of Justice
950 Pennsylvania Avenue NW
Washington, DC 20530-0001
Phone: (202) 514-2000
www.usdoj.gov

Internal Revenue Service (IRS)
Phone: (800) 829-1040, for hearing impaired: (800) 829-4059
www.irs.gov

Selective Service System (SSS)
Registration Information Office
PO Box 94638
Palatine, IL 60094-4638
Phone: (847) 688-6888, for hearing impaired: (847) 688-2567
www.sss.gov

Social Security Administration (SSA)
Office of Public Inquiries
6401 Security Boulevard
Baltimore, MD 21235
Phone: (800) 772-, for hearing impaired: (800) 325-0778
www.socialsecurity.gov or www.segurosocial.gov/espanol/

Department of State (DOS)
2201 C Street NW
Washington, DC 20520
Phone: (202) 647-4000
www.state.gov

FOR MORE INFORMATION: Visit the USCIS website at www.uscis.gov. Please also visit www.welcometousa.gov, a resource for new immigrants. Call customer service at (800) 375-5283 or (800) 767-1833 (hearing impaired). To get USCIS forms, call (800) 870-3676 or look on the USCIS website.

INDEX

ABOUT THE AUTHORS

Michael B. Dye, Esq.

Michael B. Dye is a frequent international lecturer and expert in immigration law. Mr. Dye has worked in various positions for the US government for more than fifteen years, living and working overseas in myriad locations. Mr. Dye is a former US diplomat, with extensive experience working in Asia, the Middle East, Europe, and Latin America, and has the regional expertise to break through cultural barriers and provide the comprehensive legal assistance to solve all of your immigration needs. Fluent in Spanish, he has served at the US embassy in Mexico City and has worked with numerous other US embassies and consulates worldwide.

Mr. Dye's office provides immigration assistance to potential investors seeking permanent residency in the United States, entrepreneurs seeking to establish business operations in the United States, and companies looking to expand their presence by establishing new offices in the United States.

Mr. Dye also provides consular processing assistance and advises clients from all nationalities in all visa categories. Mr. Dye is a member of the American Immigration Lawyers Association (AILA), and he is admitted to practice law in various jurisdictions, including California and the District of Columbia. Mr. Dye is an active member of the American Chamber of Commerce in Japan (ACCJ) and the American Chamber of Commerce in Singapore (AmCham Singapore).

Company: Law Office of Michael B. Dye
http://www.mikedyelaw.com

Jeremy G. Stobie, CPA

Jeremy G. Stobie is the CEO of Gray (Gray International and Gray CPA, PC) an international public accounting and compliance firm with offices in the United States, Asia, and Europe. Mr. Stobie has extensive experience in US and international taxation of multinational companies, investors, US persons living overseas and foreign investors and companies investing and moving to the United States, as well as compliance with US laws for businesses and financial institutions overseas such as the Foreign Corrupt Practices Act (FCPA) and the Foreign Account Tax Compliance Act (FATCA). Mr. Stobie is also considered a subject matter expert in EB-5 lawful source of funds accounting and documentation. Mr. Stobie lectures extensively on US taxation and compliance internationally.

Mr. Stobie has over fifteen years experience in finance, securities, and private equity and also serves as the CEO and chief compliance officer of Capital Privé Suisse SA, a Geneva, Switzerland-based fund sponsor and private wealth manager. Mr. Stobie has served as CFO, CEO, and managing partner for a myriad of domestic and international businesses over the last decade. Mr. Stobie has extensive experience operating and investing in developing and developed countries.

Mr. Stobie is a certified public accountant in the United States (Texas and Washington State), certified fraud examiner, chartered global management accountant. He is certified in financial forensics by the American Institute of Public Accountants and a chartered global management accountant. Mr. Stobie is a member of the Washington Society of Certified Public Accountants and the AICPA.

Company: Gray International, Ltd.
http://www.grayintl.com

Made in the USA
San Bernardino, CA
30 July 2015